The Capitol Story
Statehouse in Texas

(next two pages)
"State Capitol at U.T., Austin," watercolor by Mary Doerr.

The Capitol Story
Statehouse in Texas

Mike Fowler and Jack Maguire
With Noel Grisham and Marla Johnson

Eakin Press ☆ Austin, Texas

FIRST EDITION

Copyright © 1988
By Mike Fowler and Jack Maguire

Published in the United States of America
By Eakin Press, P.O. Box 23069, Austin, Texas 78735

ISBN 0-89015-663-8

Book Designer: Peggy Parkhurst

*Cover oil painting
by G. Harvey*

Library of Congress Cataloging-in-Publication Data

Fowler, Mike, 1947–
    The capitol story : the statehouse in Texas / Mike Fowler and Jack Maguire with Noel Grisham and Marla
Johnson.
        p.   cm.
    Bibliography: p.
    Includes index.
    ISBN 0-89015-663-8 : $29.95
    1. Texas State Capitol (Austin, Tex.)—History. 2. Austin (Tex.)—Buildings, structures, etc. I. Maguire,
Jack, 1919–   . II. Title.
F394.A98T484   1988
976.6′31--dc19   88-16502
                                                                CIP

Contents

Preface

Texas: A World in Itself was the unabashedly proud title that George Sessions Perry gave his rollicking portrait of the past and present of his native state when the book was published in 1942.

Perry's work underscored a fact long recognized by outsiders: Texans do have a unique pride in their homeland. The trait was born during the nine-year existence of the Republic of Texas more than a century and a half ago. That feeling of independence still exists in the unrepentantly chauvinistic hearts of modern Texans.

One outsider who understood the Texas mystique was the late John Steinbeck. In his delightful book *Travels With Charlie*, he ends his description of a visit to his wife's home state this way: "Texas is the obsession, the proper study and the passionate possession of all Texans."

In exploring the far reaches of Texas in a camper and accompanied only by his faithful dog, Steinbeck discovered a truth rarely understood by most visitors: Texans have never liked to do things in the usual way.

The magnificent Texas State Capitol is a case in point. For thirty-five years after Texas had given up its independence to join the Union, there had been a capitol in Austin. In fact, there had been two. Neither were edifices to which the former Republic could point with pride.

In 1880, however, visionary Texans decided to build a capitol that would be the envy of the nation. The state had no money, but it had more than 40 million acres of public lands. The people decided to trade more than three million acres of that asset for a grandiose statehouse.

This is the story of how they did it. But it is more than the chronicle of a building. It is the narrative of a people who, throughout their history, have always done things their way—and with pride.

Acknowledgments

This book could have been appropriately titled *To Texas with Love*. Each of those who have contributed to it are people who passionately love the Texas State Capitol. It was written for the millions of others who feel that same affection for this great red granite building.

The book was conceived by Mike Fowler, a longtime employee of the Texas House of Representatives. Fowler, along with Noel Grisham, author, educator, and former member of the Texas legislature, spent years of research and personal funds gathering information and the unique photographs that illustrate this volume. Fowler, Grisham, and Marla Johnson wrote the first and second drafts.

Jack Maguire, former executive director of The University of Texas Institute of Texan Cultures and author or co-author of six books on little-known facts about Texas history, did additional research. He is the author of the final draft.

Audray Bateman Randle of the Austin History Center, Austin Public Library, provided invaluable research and assistance and made many suggestions regarding content. Lieutenant Governor William P. Hobby, Jr., provided background material and heartily endorsed the project.

A special debt of gratitude goes to Ann Maguire, Jack's wife, for her constructive criticisms and the editing of the final manuscript. Similar appreciation is due Donna Fowler, Mike's wife, for her steadfast support and inspiration.

Most of all, we—and all Texans—are forever indebted to those who have gone before. Without those visionaries of a century ago, the magnificent edifice that is the Capitol of Texas would never have existed at all.

Photographic and Artistic Credits

Without the photographs and artwork, this would be just another book. Thanks to the unknown photographers, artists, architects, and illustrators of the past.

PHOTOGRAPHERS

Reagan Bradshaw
Mike Fowler
Gale Kloesel
Bill Malone
Tom McCormick
Barbara Schlief

ARTISTS

Present-day
Mary Doerr
G. Harvey
Bob Langkop

Deceased
William Henry Huddle
H. A. McArdle
E. E. Myers
Elisabet Ney

Special thanks are extended to Ron Whitfield, who, through his efforts and talents, helped make this book possible.

Thanks to the unknown photographers, artists, architects, and illustrators of the past.

Members of the 1906 Texas Photographers Association Convention have their portrait taken on the Capitol steps. *(Photo courtesy of Karen Thompson)*

Additional Acknowledgments

INDIVIDUALS

Clifford Beaver
Margaret Berry
T. Rodger Blythe (in memoriam)
Bill Clayton
Carol Cline
Hugh Davenport
Bess Dunlavey (in memoriam)
Aine, Emily, and Luke Fowler
Mel Fowler (in memoriam)
Vee Fowler
David Gracy
Helen Grisham
Carroll E. Gustafson
Ann Harlow
John K. Johnson
Wesley and Krista Johnson
William P. Hobby
Betty King

Gale Kloesel
John W. Kokernot (in memoriam)
Allen McCree
Tom Munnerlyn
Allen Pannell
C.H. Petri
Gaye Polan
Don Quick
Jan Rader
Jim Reynolds
Sally Reynolds
Jim Sanders
Leo Schwartz
Wade Spilman
John Stern
Karen Thompson
John M. H. Ulrich IV

ORGANIZATIONS

Austin-American Statesman
Austin-Travis County Collection, Austin History Center, City of Austin Library
Eugene C. Barker Texas History Center, The University of Texas at Austin
The Capitol Committee, Inc.
Detroit Public Library, Detroit, Michigan
The Institute of Texan Cultures, San Antonio, Texas
Office of the Governor, State of Texas
Office of the Lieutenant Governor, State of Texas
Office of the Speaker of the House, State of Texas
Office of the Attorney General, State of Texas
Panhandle-Plains Historical Museum, Canyon, Texas
State Preservation Board
State Purchasing and General Services Commission
Texas Highway Department
Texas Historical Commission
Texas House of Representatives
Texas Legislative Council
Texas Legislative Reference Library
Texas Memorial Museum, The University of Texas at Austin
Texas State Archives
Texas State Historical Association
Texas State Library
Texas State Senate

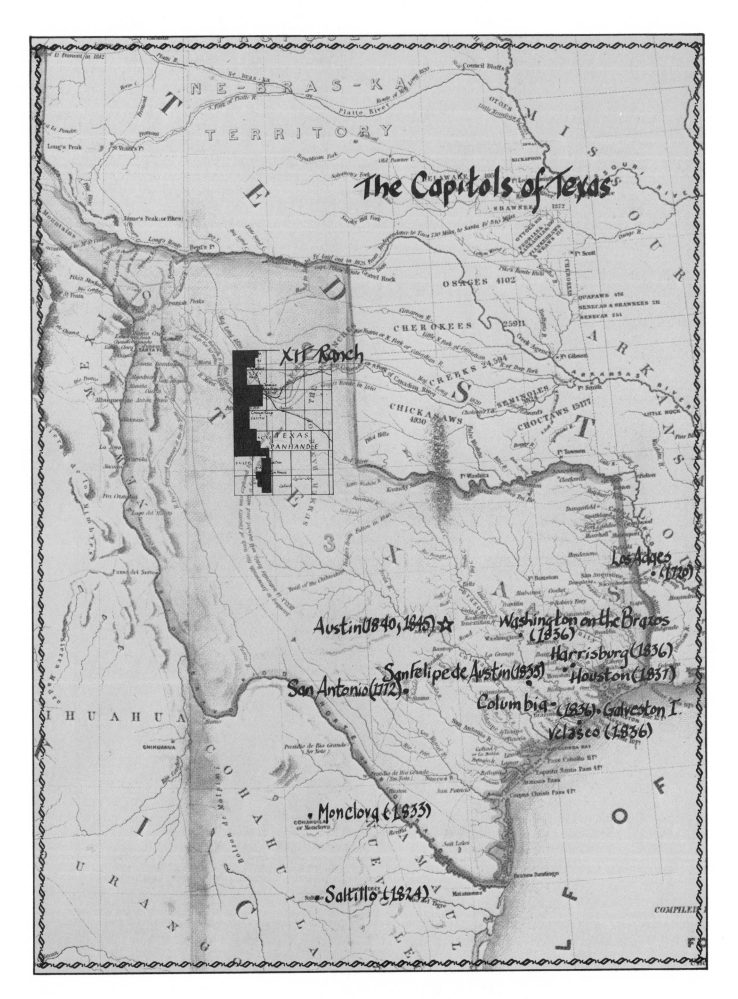

The Capitols of Texas

XIT Ranch

Los Adaes (1720)

Austin (1840, 1845) ☆

Washington on the Brazos (1836)

Harrisburg (1836)

San Felipe de Austin (1835)

Houston (1837)

San Antonio (1772)

Columbia (1836) Galveston I.

Velasco (1836)

Monclova (1833)

Saltillo (1824)

The Capitol Story
Part I

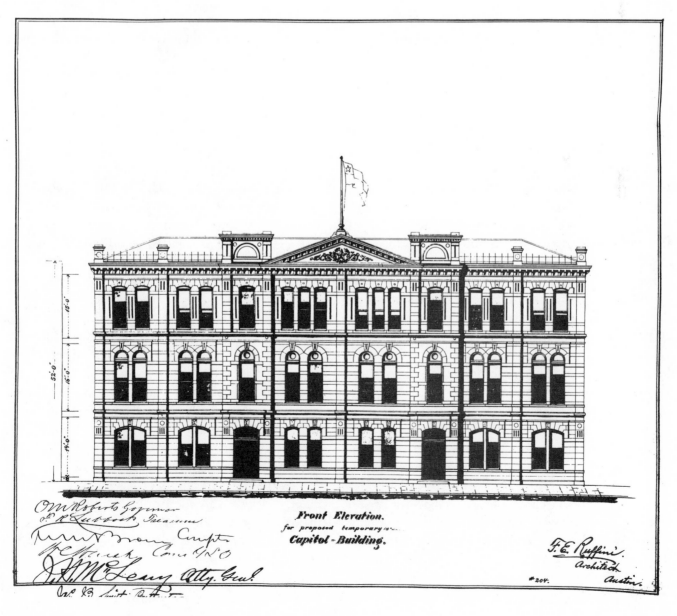

Front Elevation.
for proposed temporary
Capitol-Building.

1

The Beginnings

It was more than a century ago—February 1, 1882—that the State of Texas began building a capitol that still isn't finished. Taxpayers don't legally own the 25.96 acres of prime Austin real estate on which it sits. They do, however, own the big, red granite building with an estimated eighteen acres of floor space that makes it the largest headquarters of any state government in the Union. It is, by design, seven feet taller than the nation's Capitol.

When it was completed in 1888, the building appeared to be a bargain. Cash-poor Texas had swapped 3,050,000 acres of land worth fifty cents an acre to get a magnificent granite structure of 392 rooms, 18 vaults, 924 windows, and 404 doors. In 1988, however, this same land, worth $1.5 million a century ago, had a tax valuation of almost $7 billion. This figure would make the Texas State Capitol the most expensive government structure ever erected in the world.

Whatever its real cost, the building is something of a monument to non-Texans. It was designed by a Detroit architect and built by a Chicago syndicate. Even most of the stonemasons had to be imported from Scotland. Few such artisans lived in Texas, since the granite-quarrying industry had not begun, and members of the American stonecutters' union in other states boycotted the project.

The boycott resulted from the builder's decision to use convicts from the state prison as laborers. They were conscripted because they worked for their room and board and the chance to live outside of prison walls. Their daily wage (sixty-five cents) went to the state as payment for "leasing" its charges to the contractor.

The union masons objected not only to the "wage" paid the prisoners, but also the fact that the majority were black. Racism was a way of life, and Negroes were barred from union membership.

Once the decision was made to build, advertisements were placed in national publications in an effort to interest contractors willing to forego cash and take payment for the job. Only two contractors responded. Only one—Mattheas Schnell of Rock Island, Illinois —had no problem in posting the required $250,000 bond. The contract went to him.

Schnell, however, was not to be the builder. He sold the contract to a syndicate with enough personal capital to finance the project while hoping to turn $1.5 million worth of land into an eventual profit. The members of the syndicate knew a good thing when they saw it. They would turn the three million acres of "worthless" land into the great XIT Ranch. The XIT, which translated into "ten in Texas" because it spread over that many counties, became such a vast cattle factory that it required more than 6,000 miles of barbed wire just to fence it.

Certainly, the deal that resulted was satisfactory to both the citizens and the contractors at the time. Although the project seemed to be a bargain, it was to give Texas a government headquarters that partisans claimed was the seventh largest building ever constructed on the globe up to that time. A century after its dedication, it still stands as a testimonial to the early Texans whose dream of a glorious future is represented in its grandeur.

Although the Capitol is less functional than the glass, concrete, and aluminum skyscrapers that have dwarfed it in downtown Austin today, it was exactly what the Texans of 1882 wanted. Few questioned the economics of swapping cheap land for the grand building they envisioned. For almost half a century they had waited for a decent seat of government.

As early as 1839, when Texas was still a young and very broke independent Republic, President Mirabeau B. Lamar had named a commission to find a site for a permanent capital. The commissioners finally selected a village called Waterloo on the north bank of the Colorado River. Legend has it that Lamar thought the spot was one of the most beautiful anywhere. Congress agreed. That body approved the site on January 19, 1840, and renamed the village "Austin." It was their way of honoring Stephen F. Austin, who, in fulfilling his father's dream, had brought in the first Anglo settlers nineteen years earlier. Known even then as "the Father of Texas," he hoped that one day he might be president of the nation he had helped to found.

Shortly after Congress acted, a temporary capitol was built. It stood on a site which Austin residents years later would nickname "Kissing Hill" because it became a trysting place for young lovers. Except for courting couples, the spot was not highly regarded by most citizens of the pioneer village. The structure hardly expressed the pride Texans felt in their hard-won independence. One contemporary newspaper described the Capitol as resembling "a large-sized corn crib."

Actually, the little log structure had never been planned as anything more than a temporary arrangement. Already Texans were anticipating annexation by the United States. They knew that statehood would require a more imposing governmental headquarters. However, many doubted that Austin would be the final seat, and there were sound historical reasons for their doubts. A building does not a government make, and by 1840, Texas already had become the most over-capitalized body politic in modern times.

CAPITOLS OF TEXAS.

Composite of Texas Capitals
The Texas capital was moved many times before the current Austin site was selected in 1845. Previous Texas capitals were: Monclova, Mexico (1700); Los Adaes (now Robeline, Louisiana) (1720); San Antonio (1772); Saltillo (1824); Monclova (1833); San Felipe de Austin (1835); Washington-on-the-Brazos (1836); Harrisburg (1836); Galveston Island (1836); Velasco (1836); Columbia (1836); Houston (1837); Austin (1840); and Washington-on-the-Brazos (1842).

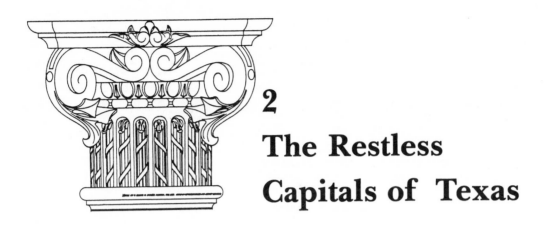

2
The Restless Capitals of Texas

Since Alonso Alvarez de Pineda arrived in 1519 to map the Gulf Coast and claim the area for Spain, Texas has moved its capital fifteen times to eleven different locations. It has boasted a capital for a longer period than any of the fifty states except Hawaii. Four communities—Austin, Houston, Monclova (Mexico), and Washington-on-the-Brazos—have each served two periods as the designated seat of government.

By one reckoning, Madrid was the first capital of Texas, beginning with Spain's claim to this New World territory. However, the area of Spanish North America that included Texas actually was governed from Mexico City. Thus, that metropolis can claim to have been the capital longer than any other.

For 162 years, what little government Texas had was conducted in the majestic National Palace of that great city some 1,000 miles south of Austin. Mexico City might have remained the seat of government even longer had not the French entered the picture. In 1682, Robert Cavelier, Sieur de La Salle, built a fort at Matagorda Bay and claimed Texas for France.

When this intelligence reached Mexico City, Alonzo de Leon, the Spanish viceroy, dispatched some soldiers north ostensibly to "survey" the area. His real purpose was to determine if the French had intentions of claiming Texas. As an added precaution, he moved the capital of the territory north to Monclova the same year.

Monclova (1682–1720; 1833–1835)

Monclova, on the river of the same name in Coahuila, is one of the oldest towns in northern Mexico. Its beginnings go back to 1577, when the settlement was called Mina de Trinidad. By 1682, when

Spain was using it as its base for further "explorations" in Texas, Monclova was a thriving community. For the next thirty-eight years, it was to be the first colonial capital.

In 1720 the French presence in Louisiana caused the Spanish authorities to move the capital again. This time it was to Los Adaes, near the present site of Robeline, Louisiana. The government was there for fifty-two years and was relocated twice more before being moved back to Monclova again in 1833.

Los Adaes (1721–1773)

Domingo Ramón's Spanish expedition of 1716 had founded the mission of San Miguel de Linares de los Adaes. In 1721, the Aguayo Expedition established a presidio there. By the time Los Adaes became the capital that same year, the settlement had a sizeable population of priests, soldiers, and civilians. Important was the fact that it was only fifteen miles west of Natchitoches, the principal base of the French.

Once the government was in place at Los Adaes, the Spanish discovered that France was hardly a threat. La Salle's expedition had been shipwrecked as he searched for the mouth of the Mississippi. He managed to get a few miles up the Lavaca River and build a small fort, primarily for defense against the Indians. Later, he and seventeen of his men were murdered by one of their own company near the present site of Navasota, and most of the others were killed by Indians.

The principal inroad by the French into Spanish Texas had been made in 1713 when Louis Juchereau St. Denis had founded Natchitoches and marched on to a Spanish outpost on the Rio Grande, the Mission San Juan Bautista. Although it was this activity that had prompted the Spanish to move the capital to Louisiana, no military action resulted. Instead, the move opened trade between the two countries, and for fifty years, Los Adaes acted as the center of commerce, diplomatic relations, and missionary activity on the eastern frontier of Spanish Texas.

San Antonio de Bexar (1771–1824)

With France no longer a threat, Spain decided to move the capital closer to Mexico City. This time it went to San Antonio de Bexar, where a presidio already existed. Also it was the site of the Mission de Valero, later to be renamed the Alamo. These institutions had made the area so important that the king of Spain decided to colonize it. In 1731 he had sent fifteen Canary Island families to establish the first European settlement in Texas. When it became the capital forty years later, it already was a bustling community of soldiers, priests, and tradesmen.

San Antonio was to be the capital for fifty-three years. When Mexico won its independence from Spain in 1821, however, the government was again moved closer to Mexico City. Saltillo became the capital of the Mexican state of Coahuila and Texas.

Saltillo (1824–1833)

One of northern Mexico's oldest towns, Saltillo, was founded in 1586 to support a mission that had been established there four years earlier. On the main road from San Antonio de Bexar to Mexico City, it seemed an ideal site from which to govern the huge geographic area that was Coahuila and Texas.

On August 15, 1824, the first session of the legislature convened. The one delegate allowed Texas, Stephen F. Austin, was absent; he would not arrive until October. That Texas was allowed only one delegate was a matter of population. Coahuila, much older and with many more residents, was allowed ten. This displeased the Texans, and in 1825 Texas was reorganized as a department and placed under a political chief headquartered in San Antonio. His assignment was to be the link between the governor at Saltillo and the political authorities in Texas.

This effort to departmentalize control was to give Texas what, in effect, became three separate governments for a period. Stephen F. Austin, whose original colony of 300 settlers was continuing to grow, was given complete civil and military control of a new Department of Brazos. At Nacogdoches, the only other settlement of importance besides Austin's colony and San Antonio, a similar department was set up.

Austin, grateful to Mexico for his original land grant and the honor of being Texas's first *empresario,* used his clout for political advantage. He required each of his colonists to swear allegiance to Mexico and become at least nominal converts to the Roman Catholic Church.

Political differences arise in every government, and that of Coahuila and Texas was no exception. The passage of an anti-immigration law by the national government in 1830 was destined to give Texans the same stimulus to revolt that the Stamp Act had given the American colonists in 1776. When convicts were sent to help the military build a string of presidios to enforce the law, the anger of the colonists only increased.

Tension continued to grow, especially at Anahuac, when promised land titles weren't issued and slaves of the settlers were impressed to work for the government without pay. When some of the dissenters were arrested and jailed, other residents reacted. Known as the "Anahuac Disturbances," these actions were the first signs of open revolt by the colonists.

The response from Mexico City was to order the capital of Coahuila and Texas moved back to Monclova. Meanwhile the Texans had called a convention of their own to meet at San Felipe de Austin.

San Felipe de Austin (1831–1835)

Although that was never the intent, the calling of the convention at San Felipe effectively made that place rather than Monclova the real capital of Texas. The official government remained in the Mexican city and the affairs of Coahuila were administered from there. But all decisions affecting the future of Texas, including the eventual revolt against Mexico, were made at San Felipe in the two Conventions of 1831 and 1833 and the Consultation of 1835.

When the consultation met there on November 6, 1835, to debate the issue of revolt versus conciliation, the delegates voted 33 to 15 to try to resolve their differences with Mexico. However, they also declared San Felipe the *de facto* capital of Texas. Citizens of the principal settlement in Austin's colony hoped that San Felipe would eventually become the permanent capital of Texas, but this was not to be.

Their dream might have become a reality if it had not been for Sam Houston, who never seemed to be satisfied with the locations of the Texas government. When another convention was called seventy-two days after the San Felipe consultation, Houston insisted, over the protests of the majority of the delegates, that it meet at Washington-on-the-Brazos.

Washington-on-the-Brazos (1836)

The upstart hamlet of Washington, with fewer than 100 residents, had no building large enough to hold the fifty-nine delegates. The only sleeping accommodations were in the homes of citizens. There wasn't even a printing press available to disseminate the deliberations of the delegates.

Despite such a lack of amenities, the convention met on March 1, 1836, with a single agenda item: the writing of a declaration of independence. A howling blue norther arrived the same day, and the bone-chilling cold may have inspired the delegates to write and sign that historic document in only three days.

Once the declaration was completed, the delegates stayed on to draw up a new constitution for the Republic of Texas, name Sam Houston as commander-in-chief of the army, and form an *ad interim* government. While they were completing their work, the Alamo fell on March 6. This did not deter the new nation from its path to independence, and the convention completed its work ten days later.

At 2:00 A.M. on March 17, the delegates adjourned after inaugurating a Yankee lawyer named David G. Burnet as the interim president of the new government. For vice-president, the delegates chose Lorenzo de Zavala, a distinguished native of Mexico. One of the first acts of the new chief executive was to choose a new capital.

Harrisburg (1836)

In proclaiming the new location for his government, Burnet insisted that "the removal is not the result of any apprehension that the enemy is near [Washington-on-the-Brazos]." He chose Harrisburg (now a part of Houston) because it was near the coast, and incoming ships could be relied on for supplies and communications. The president and his cabinet reached there on March 22.

The new nation was not to be headquartered long in Harrisburg. Santa Anna, flushed with victory at the Alamo and at Goliad, set out to capture Burnet and his government. Scouts got word to Harrisburg that the Mexicans were coming, and on April 14 and 15 Burnet was on the move again.

Writing of this experience, Burnet said: "The government of Texas was locomotive, as on wheels, moving from place to place, with no fixed abode and without decent shelter for the official family."

Galveston (1836)

It took six days for President Burnet and key members of his government to sail to Galveston. From the island haven, Burnet could do little except wonder where Sam Houston and his soldiers were. For more than a month, Houston and his rag-tag, ill-trained, ill-equipped soldiers had been in retreat. Burnet's orders to stop and fight had been ignored.

On April 19, Houston reached San Jacinto—the farthest point that he could go. Desertions had reduced his force to 800 men. Two small cannon, gifts of the people of Cincinnati, Ohio, were his only artillery. Santa Anna and his Mexican army of 700 were already camped nearby, and more than 500 reinforcements would arrive before Houston could attack.

Houston waited until 4:30 P.M. on April 21. While the Mexicans were at *siesta* and Santa Anna dallied with a beautiful mulatto girl in his tent, the Texans attacked. Advancing in a long line only two ranks deep, their marching song was a bawdy Irish ballad, "Will You Come to the Bower?", played by a four-piece band. In only eighteen minutes, the Texans killed 630 enemy soldiers, captured 730 others (including Santa Anna himself), and won forever the independence of Texas. Houston's little army suffered only ten casualties.

The victory at San Jacinto did nothing, however, to endear Sam Houston to President Burnet. Nine years after independence, and after Houston had served two terms himself as president of the Republic, Burnet wrote:

> Sam Houston has been generally acclaimed as the hero of San Jacinto. No fiction of the novelist is farther from the truth. Houston was the only man on the battlefield who deserved censure. The army regarded him as a military fop, and the citizens were disgusted with his miserable imbecility. But Sam Houston, never worthy to be called a brave man or a wise man, became the hero of San Jacinto and the second President of the Republic.

Burnet did, however, go to San Jacinto to congratulate the troops and take personal charge of Santa Anna. Then on May 8, he again announced that he was moving the capital—this time to Velasco.

Velasco (1836)

Velasco, a kind of crude summer resort at the mouth of the Brazos River on the mainland, offered more amenities than did Galveston Island. Burnet made it his headquarters from May until September. It was here on May 14 that Santa Anna, in exchange for his life, signed the treaty in which he agreed to obtain official recognition from Mexico of the independence of Texas.

By late summer, Burnet realized that Velasco lacked the facilities for a proper seat of government. When Columbia (now West Columbia) offered quarters rent-free to the Republic, Burnet ordered the capital moved there.

Columbia (1836)

At least Columbia had a two-story building, formerly a grocery, that allowed ample space for the fourteen senators and twenty-nine members of the Congress to meet. There also was a printing press, a luxury that had not been available to the government since Washington-on-the-Brazos.

The first Congress of the Republic met there on October 3, 1836. The lawmakers who convened that pleasant fall morning must have been as curious over the circumstances that brought them together as they were excited over their role in building a new nation from scratch. Only a year earlier, the representative body of Texas was a provincial government of Mexico. Not many years before, many of these same citizens had sworn allegiance to the king of Spain. Now they had gathered to create a permanent government for the fledgling Republic of Texas.

The responsibility had descended upon a unique group. Francisco Ruiz of Bexar was the only native Texan among the fourteen senators. Most of the others were immigrants from the United States. Six of the fourteen had signed the Declaration of Independence, and four had fought at San Jacinto. Having declared the freedom of Texas and won it in battle, their challenge now was to govern the nation they had helped to create.

First item of business for the Congress was the election of successors to the *ad interim* officers. As was expected, Sam Houston was chosen president and Mirabeau B. Lamar was named vice-president. Stephen F. Austin, who wanted to be chief executive, agreed to be Houston's secretary of state. The new officers were inaugurated and the Congress turned its attention to selecting what the members believed would be the permanent capital of Texas.

Washington-on-the-Brazos, which had served once as the seat of government, was a leading contender. So was Matagorda. A village on the Colorado River that would one day be known as Austin didn't even exist. The final choice of a capital would be the work of two brothers from upstate New York who were anxious to make some money out of a real estate deal.

August C. and John K. Allen were determined to transform a barren spot on the Texas coast into a profitable land speculation deal. When they gave the place the magical name of "Houston," their success was assured. With old Sam's enthusiastic blessing, the Congress picked Houston as the permanent capital of Texas.

Houston (1836–1839; 1842)

The Allen brothers tried to make their "nonexistent" town into a suitable capital. As promised, they built a two-story statehouse at what is now the corner of Houston's Main Street and Texas Avenue (later the site of the Rice Hotel). They also put up a "mansion" for the president — a two-room log house with dirt floors. The secretary of the treasury had to function in an open shed. Members of Congress were forced to stand when they met because their chambers had no chairs.

Under these circumstances, it was not surprising that the leaders of the Republic were unhappy with their permanent seat of government. On October 24, 1836, the Congress directed President Houston to appoint a three-member commission to find still another site. A month later, the commissioners reported that they had not been successful.

On December 14, Houston appointed another commission to continue the search and report back by April 14, 1838. Houston personally opposed any move; he hoped that the capital of Texas would always be in the place that bore his name. But Houston's successor to the presidency, Mirabeau B. Lamar, was never a fan of the hero of San Jacinto. He became the leader of the faction to find a new site for the government's headquarters.

That site would be a tiny hamlet on the Colorado River named Waterloo, but the selection would not keep old Sam from moving the government back to Houston once again before the government finally settled permanently in Austin.

(ulhp)
Old photograph identified as Washington-on-the-Brazos with two men on horseback and others on foot. Washington-on-the-Brazos was located on the stream Los Brazos de Dios (Arms of God). It became the birthplace of the Republic of Texas with the signing of the Texas Declaration of Independence and the constitution. On March 1, 1836, delegates to a convention met at Washington-on-the-Brazos and on March 2, 1836, the Texas Declaration of Independence was signed containing these words: "We, therefore, the delegates . . . of the people of Texas . . . do hereby resolve and declare that our political connection with the Mexican nation has forever ended; and that the people of Texas do now constitute a free, sovereign and independent republic . . ."

(llhp)
The old Capitol at Columbia on the Brazos, taken on January 23, 1900, before the building was destroyed by the storm of 1900. The government met here in October 1836 for only three months. One of the first pieces of business was to select a new location for the government in Houston.

(this page)
Sketch of the Capitol of Texas at Houston City. Not surprisingly, President Sam Houston was instrumental in the government being located at his namesake. Houston City was conceived and developed by the Allen brothers, Augustus and John. When Congress arrived in April of 1837, the tiny hamlet was not prepared and the session was postponed. The Houston Capitol was erected under the supervision of Col. Thomas Ward. This structure contained twenty-two rooms and was built in the record time of fourteen days.

The Capitol of Texas at Houston City. Located on the northwest corner of Texas Avenue and Main Street. In May of 1837, Houston became the capital of the Republic of Texas and remained so until early 1840, when Congress approved Austin as the new site for the capital on January 19, 1840.

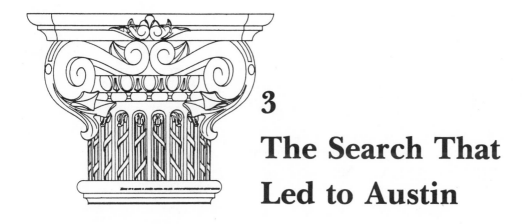

3

The Search That Led to Austin

The second commission to find a permanent site for the capital went to work with a will. They examined twelve possible locations, including San Antonio, Bastrop, San Felipe, Nacogdoches, Richmond, Washington-on-the-Brazos, and Groce's Retreat. From the beginning, there was a concensus that the capital should be located in Central Texas, and following that notion, the commission finally chose a site just below La Grange in Fayette County.

The league of land owned by John Eblin seemed to be the perfect spot, situated on a high bluff fronted by a mile and a half of the Colorado River. It was within easy travel of San Antonio, Houston, and other important settlements. And while it was not as close to the geographical center of Texas as some preferred, it was the best location the commission had found. A contract to buy the land from Eblin was drawn, and this encouraged other landowners in the area to offer their properties to the government.

Congress met on May 9, 1838, to hear the commission's report. It took only two ballots to approve Eblin's league as the site of the permanent capital. However, when the proposal reached President Houston, he vetoed it. He was undoubtedly miffed because the commission had not picked his beloved Houston, but he based his objections on other grounds.

In his veto message, he reminded the lawmakers that the act locating the temporary capital on Buffalo Bayou had specified that it would remain there through the session of Congress in 1840. He also pointed out that moving the capital would not save money, as some members argued, but actually would be much more expensive. Congress reacted by attempting to overturn his veto, but failed. As a result, the matter of a new capital was set aside for a time.

Lamar Wins His Point

When Mirabeau B. Lamar was sworn in as president on December 10, 1838, he had already decided where he wanted the new capital located. Earlier he had been on a hunting trip along the Colorado River and discovered a tiny settlement called Waterloo on the east bank. Entranced by the surrounding hills to the west and the rich farm lands to the east, he envisioned this as the future headquarters of the Republic.

From an economic standpoint, Lamar's opponents probably were correct in wanting to keep Houston as the capital. In fact, thirteen years after the decision was made to make Austin the headquarters of the government, one nationally known economist was still arguing that the move should never have happened. This prominent Philadelphia banker, William Gouge, contended that moving the capital to Austin was nothing more than a boondoggle sponsored by early land developers anxious to make a fast buck.

Gouge never had any direct connection with either the Republic of Texas or the state it later became, but he had a lasting interest in its economic development. In 1852 he published a book titled *The Fiscal History of Texas from the Commencement of the Revolution in 1834 to 1851–52*. In it he suggested, among other things, that Texas owed its existence to a pig (see Chapter 12). And he believed that the move of the capital to Austin was contrived by real estate speculators:

> The removal [of the capital] was an act of pure folly, as it increased the expenditures of both the governors and the governed, but it afforded the opportunity of speculating on the sale of lots in

the new metropolis and it invited speculation on lands in the interior. And these two motives combined were too strong to be resisted.

Gouge's opposition to the move came thirteen years too late to have any effect on the decision. The voices of other opponents were ignored. With Lamar's backing, Congress did not delay. An "Act for the Permanent Location for the Seat of Government" was quickly passed and signed by the president on January 14, 1839. It called for the appointment of still another commission and instructed it to select a site "between the rivers Trinidad and Colorado, and above the Old San Antonio Road." The latter crossed the Colorado at Bastrop.

Members of Congress hoped that public lands could be found for the site, which the act specified as being not less than one or more than four leagues in size. If the land was not publicly owned, the commission was to encourage the private owners to donate it. Failing that, the commissioners were authorized to buy a single league if it cost no more than three dollars an acre. Finally, if none of these options were found, the commission was directed to ask the courts to condemn it and deed it to the Republic.

If the land was to be taken by condemnation, the owner would be notified, a jury would determine the fair value, and the commissioners would pay the amount awarded with drafts on the national treasury. The land thus would be owned in perpetuity by the Republic of Texas.

As early as October 11, 1837, the highly respected *Telegraph and Texas Register,* the state's leading newspaper, published an anonymous letter suggesting the building of a capital city that would be promoted and controlled by the public. The idea of finding vacant acreage and creating a seat of government on it was not new. Washington, D.C., already stood as an example of what could be done with a planned city.

Such an idea may have been in President Lamar's mind when he got Congress to incorporate the settlement of Waterloo on January 15, 1839, only a day after he had signed the act directing the commission to find a location for the permanent capital. His rush to incorporate Waterloo seemed a clear signal that this was the site he preferred.

Only four families were resident there at the time. They were settled on the banks of the Colorado near where Congress Avenue crosses the river today. Isolated, and with not even the meager amenities that Houston and the other temporary capitals had offered, Waterloo seemed an unlikely site for the headquarters of a new nation. Lamar, however, dreamed that thousands would live there one day, and he saw to it that the little settlement be renamed "Austin."

A Permanent Capital at Last

By March 23, 1839, the selection of the capital site was finalized. The commissioners notified the Bastrop County court that they had chosen "five thirds of leagues of land, and two labors of land, situated, lying, and being in, the county of Bastrop on the east bank of the Colorado River." This tract, now a part of the city of Austin, is marked by Springdale Road on the east, West Lynn and North Lamar on the west, and the river on the south. The northern boundary is irregular since some of the acreage was in varying widths.

The Republic of Texas, following the pattern of its neighboring nation to the north, had selected a beautiful unpopulated site on which it would build a city specifically planned as the seat of government. In the intervening decades since, however, Austin somehow lost the careful planning still evident in the nation's capital.

President Lamar, anxious to get the new town platted and the lots sold, appointed Edwin Waller, a Brazoria County surveyor, as the Republic's land agent. He was given only until October 1 to lay out the townsite. By that date, President Lamar also wanted a Capitol constructed, a house built for the chief executive, and all other necessary buildings ready for occupancy.

Platting went rapidly. The townsite would be fourteen blocks square, with certain areas designated for public buildings, squares, churches, and businesses. Four square blocks in the north central section were reserved as the site of the Capitol. Other public buildings were to be located in surrounding half blocks.

On August 1 the first lots were auctioned; 217 were sold at prices ranging from $120 to $2,700. The sale generated $300,000, but it did little to add cash to the Republic's faltering treasury. The terms of the sale were so generous that it was years before the government finally got most of its money.

Meanwhile, Waller faced the almost impossible task of getting the needed buildings ready for the arrival of the government. Materials were virtually nonexistent in the immediate area, the nearest sawmill being miles to the east. Necessities like glass, hardware, and even the better timbers had to be brought by wagon from Houston. Since there were no laborers in Austin, workers had to be imported from distant settlements. They were disgruntled by the short supply of food and having to work in the almost unbearable heat. Indian raids were a constant concern.

In spite of these problems, Waller accomplished something of a construction miracle. When he found it almost impossible to obtain milled lumber, he substituted post oak logs for most of the buildings. Other logs came from the "lost pines" at Bastrop, thirty-five miles of rough wagon road away. Shakes cut from the abundant native cedars and cypress trees were used for roofing.

The Capitol was located on the present site of the city's municipal building. It fronted east toward Congress for 110 feet and was 50 feet deep. A central hall provided a chamber for the House on one side and one for the Senate on the other. Shed rooms on the west side were for committee meetings. On the west was another building which offered cots for sleeping, a kitchen, and a dining room. Since Indians were ever present, the entire area was protected by a stockade.

On the east side of Congress Avenue, and facing the Capitol entrance, was the log house of the quartermaster general. Buildings housing the State and Navy departments and the vice-president of the Republic were just south of the Capitol on the west side of Congress. Structures for the Land Office, Postmaster General, and other government functions were located at various points along the avenue to Fourth Street. The President's Mansion was a two-story structure between the present Seventh and Eighth streets.

On September 1, 1839, the government began its official move from Houston to Austin with the transfer of the archives. Although the Republic of Texas had been in existence only forty months, it had generated lots of paper. More than forty freight wagons were needed to transport the government's documents, plus some meager furniture for the offices. President Lamar and his cabinet arrived a month later.

On the second Monday in November, the government went to work officially in its new location when the Fourth Congress convened in the rustic Capitol. There, on November 12, Lamar welcomed the lawmakers, apologized for the privations, and urged his colleagues to adjust to the new environment. The president was lavish in his praise of the new capital site, but many members of the Congress were not. They felt that the people should have the final word

as to where their government should be headquartered.

Almost immediately after Congress convened, a bill was introduced to call a public election so the people could decide. Although it had substantial support, the bill was defeated. Austin, for better or worse, was the "official" capital of the Republic. For years, however, some members of Congress and other officials always referred to the site on the Colorado as the "temporary" capital.

This jest almost proved prophetic. In the 1841 elections, Sam Houston was reelected president. He had opposed the Austin location from the start and often described it as "the most unfortunate site on earth for a Seat of Government." As the new head of state, he showed his disdain for both the capital and his predecessor in office by refusing to attend Lamar's farewell "gala" at the President's Mansion. Once he was inaugurated, Houston took a room in a boardinghouse rather than occupy the official residence.

His return to the presidency only intensified his desire to have the government vacate Austin. In his inaugural address, he urged Congress to pass a bill that would move the capital back to Houston. The measure was defeated, but Houston wasn't. In March 1842, a Mexican army invaded Texas and captured San Antonio, Goliad, and Victoria. The president convened a special session of Congress to discuss the emergency, but he called the legislators to meet in Houston, not Austin. He argued that the capital was defenseless against a Mexican attack.

The Archives War

Houston's opponents believed, probably with good reason, that the move out of Austin was prompted by his selfish desire to headquarter the government in his namesake town. His argument was that the Republic's archives would be in danger of capture by the invading Mexicans if they remained in Austin. He ordered the secretary of state to remove them to Houston.

This action set off what is known as the Archives War, when Austin citizens elected to fight rather than see the records switched to Houston.

The "war" began with the formation of a vigilante committee of residents. This committee warned the heads of each governmental department that remained in Austin not to leave. They were told that if they did attempt to move any of their official papers to Houston, they would be met with armed resistance.

To avoid a confrontation, President Houston decided to delay his plans to move the archives. But he let all of Texas know that he planned to ignore Austin as the official capital. When he called the Seventh Congress into session, he directed it to meet at Washington-on-the-Brazos. At the same time, he ordered officials and department heads to bring all their records with them.

Once the Congress had convened in December 1842, Houston decided it was time for action. Announcing that Austin was no longer the capital, he ordered Col. Thomas I. Smith and Capt. Eli Chandler to proceed immediately to Austin and retrieve the archives.

Equipped with three wagons and twenty soldiers, they managed to get past a lookout that the Austin vigilantes had posted at Bastrop, and were able to enter the capital without incident. In fact, they had almost finished loading the records when they were spotted by President Houston's erstwhile landlady, Mrs. Angelina Eberly.

The alert Mrs. Eberly immediately sounded an alarm by firing a tiny cannon that had been readied in case armed defense of the archives became necessary. She directed her blast toward the Land Office, where the records were housed. Her shot did little damage and injured nobody, but it forced the invaders to flee to the north with their wagons.

Two dozen vigilantes got a late start but began a pursuit. They overtook the soldiers at Kenney's Fort on Brushy Creek (Williamson County) on January 1, 1843. After a few shots were fired, Houston's men gave up the archives to avoid bloodshed. The would-be thieves were returned to Austin along with the records, and the citizens welcomed them with a New Year's party.

Thus the Archives War was ended, but it didn't bring the capital back to Austin. Houston kept the government at Washington while the population of Austin, its principal business gone, declined steadily.

The situation was not to last, however. On December 8, 1844, Anson Jones succeeded Houston as president. Although he continued to operate the government from Washington while bats, vermin, and even goats roamed the Capitol at Austin, Jones was responsive to political pressure. When Austin's dwindling citizenry petitioned the new president, he called the Convention of 1845 to meet there. It was a most important assemblage because its job was to draft the ordinance of annexation and draw up a new constitution for the proposed new state of Texas.

The convention was the shot in the arm that the deteriorating former capital needed. Delegates assembled in July, worked through August, and brought the town to life again. Apparently they liked the surroundings, because they saw to it that the proposed constitution specified Austin as "the present seat of government."

The delegates hedged their political bets, however, by ordering that Austin be the designated capital only until 1850. At that time, the seat of government would be "permanently located by the people."

With annexation approved by both the convention and the Congress of the Republic, the proposed new constitution was accepted by the people. Then, on December 29, 1845, the U.S. Congress voted Texas into the Union. The transfer of authority from the Republic to the new state was not concluded until February 16, 1846.

On February 19, Austin was the site where the first governor, James Pinckney Henderson, and his lieutenant governor, Albert C. Horton, took their oaths of office. And it was there that Anson Jones, the last president of the Republic of Texas, lowered that nation's flag for the last time.

Austin, at last, had become the capital of the state of Texas. In 1850, as the Congress and the Convention of 1845 had promised, Texans had an opportunity to vote on where they wanted their seat of government to be. Austin won by a large majority.

But the specter that the Capitol itself might one day disappear still hung over Austin. That possibility had arisen even before Sam Houston became president of the Republic and moved the government back to Houston. There was concern then, as there is today, that Texas never legally owned the land on which it has built four capitols in the city of Austin. That possibility, remote though it may be after a century and a half of litigation, still casts a cloud over the Capitol today.

Sketch of Austin. This artist's rendition was copied from the frontispiece of *A History of Texas, or the Emigrant's Guide to the New Republic*, published in 1840. The location of the first, and subsequent, Austin capitols was decided by Mirabeau B. Lamar, hero of the Texas Revolution and third president of the Republic. In a trip through the Hill Country west of what would become Austin, Lamar stood on a high hill surveying the area. The high hill would later be named Mt. Bonnell. From that spot, Lamar looked down upon the small community of Waterloo and chose the highest, most prominent spot to be "capitol hill." Lamar's executive home is on the hill in the right section of the drawing. The Capitol is the long building on the left side of Congress Avenue (the wide road in the middle).

Drawing of Austin about 1839 or 1841. From March 2, 1836, when the independence of Texas was declared, to January 1839, there was no permanently located seat of government. Temporarily, Houston was the capital. But due to its lack of protection to the families in the interior, President Lamar passed an act which provided a commission to select a site for the location of the capital between the Trinity and the Colorado rivers and above the old San Antonio Road. The act provided for the appointment of an agent whose duty was to have 640 acres of land selected and laid out in town lots. The community of Waterloo was selected by one vote over Salado. A sufficient number of the most eligible lots was kept for the capital, arsenal, and the university. The act provided "that the name of said site shall be Austin." Waterloo was renamed in honor of Stephen F. Austin, who had established the first Anglo colony in Texas in 1824. President Lamar arrived in 1839. In November the first session of the Fourth Congress met at the new capital. In a year's time the city government was established with Judge Edwin Waller as mayor.

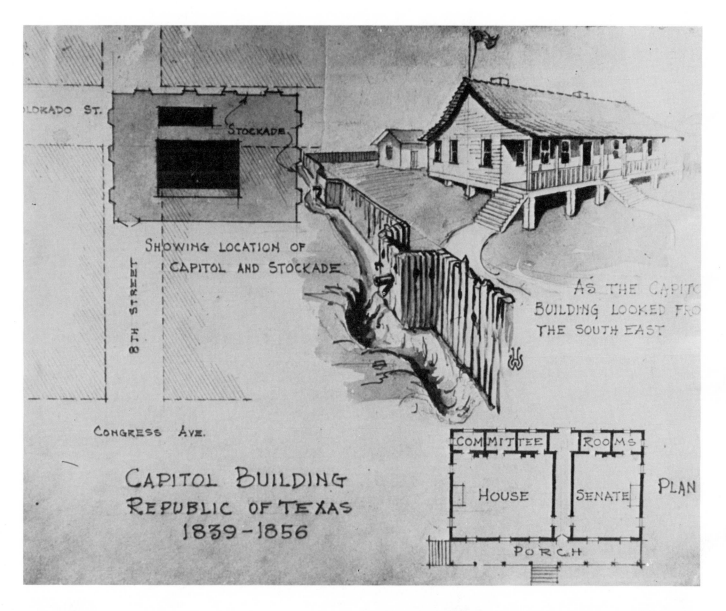

COLORADO ST.

8TH STREET

STOCKADE

SHOWING LOCATION OF
CAPITOL AND STOCKADE

CONGRESS AVE.

CAPITOL BUILDING
REPUBLIC OF TEXAS
1839-1856

AS THE CAPITO
BUILDING LOOKED FRO
THE SOUTH EAST

COMMITTEE   ROOMS

HOUSE   SENATE   PLAN

PORCH

Drawing of the Capitol building in Austin from 1839 to 1856. An eight-foot stockard stood around the first Austin state-house as a precaution against Indians. Note the arrangement of the House, Senate, and committee rooms. The February 12, 1888, *Daily Statesman* described a "frame building upon the present site of the city hall, which was enclosed in a stockade, another frame structure on the opposite hill for the executive mansion, and log cabins convenient on either side for the heads of departments . . . The location was beautiful, and the capitol of the Republic, naturally attracted a good class of people, whose peace, however, was not infrequently disturbed by raids of Indians."

MRS. EBERLEY FIRING OFF CANNON.

Mrs. Eberly firing the cannon during the main event of the famous "Archives War." In 1842, Gen. Sam Houston was determined to remove the archives from Austin to Houston, but the citizens of Austin were determined that they remain at the Capitol. The "Archives War" resulted.

Only building to be used as the Capitol for the governments of both the Republic of Texas and the State of Texas. This Capitol was located on the corner of Eighth (then known as Hickory) and Colorado streets in Austin.

Lowering of the flag of the Republic by President Anson Jones at the annexation of Texas to the United States on February 19, 1846. President Jones said, "The Lone Star of Texas, which ten years since arose amid clouds, over fields of great destruction, has now passed on and become fixed forever in that glorious constellation which all free men and lovers of freedom in the world must reverence and adore, the American Union. Blending its rays with its sister stars, long may it continue to shine ... The final act in this great drama is now performed — the Republic of Texas is no more."

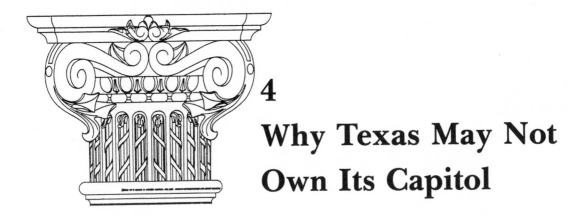

4
Why Texas May Not Own Its Capitol

No legal authority questions the fact that the state of Texas owns the huge red granite Capitol that stands at the head of Congress Avenue in Austin. Trading three million acres of West Texas lands to pay for the building's construction may not have been the best use of resources at the time, but it got the state the headquarters it wanted. While the ownership of the building is a fact, the state never has had clear title to the land on which it stands—even though it has paid for it three times.

The question of who really owns the land occupied by the Capitol goes back to the days when Mexico ruled Texas. At that time, Mexico had a quaint custom of allowing its court justices to take their pay either in cash or real estate. One of these justices was Thomas Jefferson Chambers, a colorful and controversial figure who later would hold the rank of general when Texas revolted against Mexico.

In 1834, however, he was esteemed by leaders in the Mexican government. He had earlier been given an *empresario* contract to introduce 800 new settlers into Texas. That contract was never fulfilled, but he was named superior judge of Texas in April 1834. That made him eligible to take his pay in either pesos or acreage.

Chambers, a promoter who realized that new settlers could only make Texas land values increase, elected to take his fees in real estate. Mexico was unusually generous in his case. Although he never served as judge (disorders incident to the removal of the capital from Saltillo to Monclova made it impossible for him to organize a court), he was very well paid for trying. Mexico awarded him thirty leagues, or approximately 137,268 acres of prime Texas land.

The huge tract awarded Chambers by Mexico started on the north bank of the Colorado River on the western outskirts of what now is the city of Austin. It extended thirteen miles northeast to a point just below Round Rock in Williamson County. The tract's western boundary ran south, back to the river, and through the eastern edge of today's Austin. The acreage included the land where the Capitol now stands.

Since these Mexican land grants were later guaranteed by the Republic of Texas, Chambers was in no hurry to record the title to his property. All of the tract was located in Bastrop County at the time (Travis and Williamson counties were not carved out until later), and he should have recorded the title in the Bastrop Land Office. His failure to do so is the basis for Texas's current debate over who really owns the Capitol land.

After the successful revolution in 1836, Chambers's prediction about real estate values began to come true. Land-hungry settlers poured in. The Bastrop County Land Office, having no record of the Chambers claim to any lands in the area, began granting large chunks of it to newcomers. About this same time, the Republic of Texas began searching for a permanent capital site.

By March 23, 1839, when the commission named by Congress made its selection of the current site, the commissioners also were unaware of any claim by Chambers. More than a year earlier, however, the Bastrop Land Office had patented about 1,500 acres of this same real estate to one Samuel Gocher or Goucher, a farmer living a few miles downriver. The Goucher portion included the hill where the present Capitol would be built almost half a century later.

A few months after Goucher had received the grant, his entire family was slaughtered by Indians. At least, that was thought to be the case at the time.

So with the Gouchers supposedly dead and no obvious heirs left, two real estate promoters named Edward Burleson and James Porter Brown saw a chance to turn a few dollars. They filed a claim for the Goucher property, the Land Office approved it, and Burleson and Brown sold it almost immediately to the Republic of Texas.

It was the first time Texas paid for the land where its Capitol sits. There would be others.

General Chambers Goes to Court

Meanwhile, Chambers had been living at Round Point (Liberty County) and not paying much attention to the search for a capital site. It was not until 1840 that he got around to filing his claim, only to discover that 150 separate patents had been issued to others. He immediately went on the attack, filing lawsuits against everyone who claimed any part of what he believed to be rightfully his.

The Republic of Texas, however, fell back on its constitutional right not to be sued unless the government granted its express permission. It not only refused to give such permission, but ignored Chambers's claims altogether. The government was too busy with plans to build its first permanent Capitol and was not to be deterred by Chambers or anyone else.

The general, however, with no intention of surrendering or retreating, kept his lawsuits alive. After 1845, when Texas traded its independence for $10 million and statehood, the legislature continued to refuse Chambers permission to sue. Finally, in 1858, he at least won a skirmish with the state when the Supreme Court ruled that Chambers had as perfect a title to his lands "as the law is capable of bestowing."

This did not encourage the state government to admit it was wrong, though, and Chambers continued his legal fight. That ended on March 15, 1865, when he was killed by an assassin's bullet as he sat in the library of his home, "Chambersea," at Anahuac in the Gulf Coast county named for him. He was holding his six-month-old daughter, Stella, on his knee when he was shot.

Stella and her older sister, Katie, would grow up and continue the battle for the title to the Chambers lands for another sixty years. Before they were old enough to carry on the fight, however, the Goucher claim on the capital site was resurrected.

The Gouchers Rise Again

Not all of the Gouchers had been murdered by the Indians after all. Three of the Goucher children had been kidnapped, later ransomed, and had grown up unaware that their father had patented a tract of land near their old home. A daughter, Jane, married, bore some children, and died about 1850. A son, James, died in 1849 without ever taking a bride. Another son, William, was alive in 1853 when one E. M. Smith discovered the Goucher claim. Like Burleson and Brown, who first sold the claim to the Republic in 1839, Smith saw a way to collect again from the state.

He approached William Goucher, the last known survivor, who not only was unaware of his father's land grant but also was poor and illiterate. Smith offered him $500 for a quitclaim deed to the property — a lot of money at the time for a mere 1,500 acres. William took the cash and signed the deed with his mark.

Smith, a valid deed to the acreage in hand, persuaded the legislature to permit him to sue the state for the condemnation award approved by the Congress of the Republic when its commission was out buying or condemning land for the capital. Before the case could get into court, however, the Civil War intervened. Smith's claim would not be adjudicated until April 1, 1867.

The courts took five more years to decide the issue. On June 22, 1872, a ruling was handed down to the effect that Smith did have a valid claim to the land on which the Capitol stands. In 1874 the legislature authorized payment of the judgment, and all of Texas breathed easier. Having paid for the land twice, the lawmakers believed that there was no longer a question about who owned it.

Apparently, they had forgotten about the Chambers claim. His daughters had not.

Sweet Ladies Who Claimed the Capitol

The daughters, now Mrs. Stella McGregor and Mrs. Kate Sturgis of Galveston, had filed their first legal action in 1884. Although still denied permission by the legislature to sue the state, the sisters had served a legal notice that improvements were being built on land they had inherited. They contended that these improvements would become their property automatically. Their legal skirmishing didn't result in any action by the state, but it did get the attention and win the friendship of James Stephen Hogg who, in 1886, would become the Texas attorney general.

Although there was nothing Hogg could do legally, either as the state's principal lawyer or, after 1891, as governor, his sympathies were with the sisters. On one occasion, he told them: "Build a log cabin on the Capitol grounds, move in and Jim Hogg will defend you in any legal action brought by the state."

The gentle ladies were averse to becoming actors in such a spectacular proceeding as suggested by Governor Hogg, but they never gave up the fight. They accumulated a formidable portfolio of evidence over decades of litigation and delivered it in 1924 to R. E. Cofer, a prominent Austin lawyer. He wrote later that he thought he was dealing with a couple of eccentrics when the "two sweet old ladies . . . said they owned the Texas Capitol and its grounds."

His attitude changed quickly when he had looked at the documents they brought him. "I had not read 30 minutes until I realized that these women just as certainly owned the Capitol grounds as I owned my own home," he wrote in the October 1931 issue of the *Texas Law Review*.

When the 39th Legislature convened in January, Cofer was ready to present the ancient case of the two sisters again. This time the arguments presented by Cofer and the attorneys assisting him were persuasive. Senator John Davis of Dallas was won over early. In the debate, he warned his colleagues that "Chambers' daughters could come marching up Capitol Hill with the sheriff in front, armed with a writ of possession, to take over the Capitol. In my judgment as a lawyer, the state has a chance to settle a dangerous claim for a small sum."

And a small sum it was, considering the value today of the twenty-five acres on which the Capitol sits. For only $20,000, the sisters agreed to deed the Capitol and its grounds to the state of Texas in perpetuity.

No, Texas Still Isn't the Owner

After payments to three sets of claimants, the title to the land on which Texas built its Capitol remains unclear. Experts in real estate law and abstractors agree that there is still a possibility for descendants of Samuel Goucher to come forward and make a valid claim. There are some sound reasons for this theory.

Goucher had three children, but only one son, William, signed a valid quitclaim deed. Neither James, the other son, nor Jane, the daughter, ever signed documents giving up their rights of ownership. Records show that neither was ever joined in any lawsuit regarding the claim.

Some lawyers argue that the state's award to the Chambers daughters extinguished any further claims. Also, Travis County abstracts for almost a century have begun by assuming that all land privately owned before August 1, 1839, reverted to the Republic of Texas under the power of the sovereign to condemn.

If a descendant of Jane Goucher should come forward, the validity of the claim would be difficult to prove. Even if the courts should rule that the settlement of the Chambers claim did not extinguish one that the Goucher descendants might make, it still wouldn't be an open-and-shut case. The new claimant would first have to get permission from the legislature to sue the state. Once in court, even if the claimant won, any award would not be forthcoming until the legislature appropriated the funds for payment. It was thirty-three years after the original condemnation award was made before E. M. Smith finally collected the $500 he paid William Goucher for his quitclaim deed to the same property.

In the meantime, the business of government goes on in a capitol which, although it has rendered more than a century of service, may stand on ground the state has never legally owned.

5

The First "Permanent" Capitol

Seven years after annexation of Texas by the United States, the legislature finally got around to authorizing the construction of the second, and first really permanent, capitol of the new state. The young, debt-ridden Republic had cured its fiscal problems by trading its independence for statehood and wanted to put some of its ready cash into brick (in this case, limestone) and mortar.

As a part of the annexation treaty, Texas had sold much of its lands to the United States for $10 million—enough to retire the debts of the former Republic and leave a balance of some $3 million in the treasury. In addition, the state had kept its remaining public lands—an estimated 182 million acres. Now, for the first time since independence, Texas could afford a capitol comparable to those of other members of the Union.

Population growth also was demanding the expansion of government and the necessary facility to house it. Immigration from the U.S. was constant and growing. Galveston already claimed a population of 4,177; San Antonio was second in size with 3,488. New settlements were springing up everywhere. The bustling state's new prosperity seemed to call for a proper capitol.

Serving as the fourth governor was Peter Hansborough Bell, the former Texas Ranger who always wore his hair shoulder-length and delighted in carrying two six-shooters in his belt. His long hair and rough dress made him appear to be an uncultured frontiersman with little interest in housing the government. However, like Sam Houston and others, he abhorred conducting the business of government in log cabins and was a strong supporter of a new capitol.

When the legislature passed a bill appropriating $100,000 to be "set apart for the erection of a State House or Capitol" and specifying that $25,000 of this was to be spent for "furnishing and finishing" the building, Bell quickly signed it.

The site selected was the north end of Congress Avenue on a plot designated as Capitol Square when Edwin Waller laid out the original townsite in 1839. A superintendent and two commissioners were to be appointed by the legislature to find an architect willing to provide "suitable plans for the building" at a cost not to exceed $500. They also were charged with locating a contractor who would agree to finish the job no later than November 1, 1853.

The New Capitol Takes Shape

On March 5, 1852, the firm of McGehee, Moore, Cook, and Brandon turned the first soil to begin construction of the Texas State Capitol. McGehee and Moore were the stonemasons, while Cook and Brandon were in charge of carpentry. The cornerstone was laid the following July 3. Delivering the address that day was a popular local minister, the Reverend E. Fontaine, who eloquently predicted that this "Capitol will stand erect and unscathed until the Heavens and Earth shall pass away." To the crowd that gathered for the occasion, such longevity for the proposed building seemed a possibility.

Slowly the new building rose to an imposing three stories in height, plus a basement. Fronting 140 feet on Congress Avenue, it measured 90 feet from front to rear. The exterior was soft yellow limestone, and the interior was a hard white variety of the same material. A broad stone stairway ascended from the front of the building to the second floor and an inside stair at the rear provided access to all floors.

The building was designed so that every area could be used. The basement had twelve rooms designated as offices for various departments. The main floor, decorated with marble tile laid on cement, was the nerve center of the government, with a suite for the governor and offices for the secretary of state, attorney general, adjutant general, the Education Department, and the Department of Statistics and History.

The second floor was given over to chambers for the Senate and House of Representatives and an office for the lieutenant governor. The rest of the floor consisted of committee rooms. The third floor contained the galleries of the Senate and House, plus a library and museum and offices for legislators. As a kind of afterthought, the legislature decided a courtroom for the Supreme Court was needed. On February 7, 1853, an additional appropriation of $50,000 was passed so that one could be added to the third floor.

Although construction continued on schedule, it was not without problems. A legislative committee appointed to investigate charges of irregularities and failure to comply with the law reported that the superintendent and the two commissioners selected to manage the project were not qualified. They charged that the architectural plans (for which the state had paid the magnificent sum of $500) were "defective . . useless, if not injurious." There were accusations that the contractors were incompetent to bid on the project, and that Eli Kirk, who was commissioned to buy the furnishings, could have bought the same items at less expense.

Despite the problems, the Capitol — described by one historian as "the first, fartherest West, Colonial public building in the nation" — officially became the seat of government on November 21, 1853. Although it had been described as "a building for all time to come," it was to last for only twelve days short of twenty-eight years. On November 9, 1881, it burned to the ground.

(urhp)
Southern view of the Old Stone Capitol. The foundation of this Capitol was laid in March of 1852 on a four-block square area reserved for the government. The first session held in the uncompleted building in December of 1853 was that of the Fifth Legislature, with Elisha M. Pease serving as governor.

(lrhp)
Early view of Austin with its Capitol on the skyline. During the period immediately after the Civil War, a minor problem of state government was printed in the *State Gazette* of October 12, 1867: "We understand that the Comptroller is unwilling to pay for a new carpet for the new Court . . . and that their Honor's feet may suffer from the cold before the present time is over. This is too bad. Unless their feet are kept warm and their heads cool, what sort of decisions can we expect?"

THE CAPITOL IN THE CITY OF AUSTIN.
southern view
Burned May. 8th 1881.

View of the Governor's Mansion, taken from the Old Stone Capitol about 1870. This Capitol sat on the same site that the present Capitol occupies. The building in the left corner is a Baptist church constructed about 1857.

Newspaper sketch of the interior of the Senate Chamber at the Old Stone Capitol, dated May 22, 1880. Many interesting stories surround this building. One involved an altercation between Speaker of the House Cochran and Representative Coleman on the House floor in 1879. Cochran drew a gun, but was quickly subdued. The editor of the *Daily* *Statesman* wondered what the outside world would think of their conduct: ". . . it reflects no credit upon Texas lawgivers that the Speaker of the House would allow a difference concerning parliamentary usage to lead him to arm himself with a pistol . . . It will be accepted abroad, however unjust, as an index to the character of Texas lawgivers."

Often called the "Old Stone Capitol" because of its construction of local white limestone, this building witnessed important parts of Texas history as told by Senator Temple Houston in his speech at the Capitol building dedication on May 18, 1888: "Let us not pass lightly by that old structure. Its halls knew so much of the grief and glory of Texas, so much of her splendor and sorrow . . . Beneath its roof were assembled thirteen legislatures and four constitutional conventions. There were formed the constitutions of 1861, of 1866, of 1869, and of 1876, the organic law under which we now live, . . . Within those walls, since wasted by fire, passed much over which the historian of Texas must ponder . . ."

1870 view of the ionic colonial design capitol building from the south, looking up Congress Avenue. Note that the street has not yet been paved.

1879 arch in German commemorating the twenty-fifth anniversary of the founding of the City of Austin with the Old Stone Capitol in the background. This 25th Jubilee Celebration Welcome Arch was designed by Herman Lungkwitz, a renowned German artist, in conjunction with the 1879 Staats Saengerfest.

The Old Stone Capitol as it burned November 9, 1881. S. B. Hill photographed the burning building, its dome already collapsed. The necessity for the already planned new Capitol increased dramatically with this tragedy. Ironically, at the time that the fire broke out, the Capitol Board (Governor Roberts, Comptroller Brown, Treasurer Lubbock, Land Commissioner Walsh, Col. L. N. Norton, Attorney McLeary, and the new capitol commissioner, Judge Jo Lee) was in session in the House of Representatives chamber of the Old Stone Capitol. According to the *Texas Siftings*, Governor Roberts first thought the fire was "an organized attempt to rob the treasury and immediately ordered the Rangers camped in the yard to be put on guard duty around that 'cash balance.'"

(left)
The last Senate composite photograph showing the Old Stone Capitol, SEVENTEENTH LEGISLATURE OF 1881–1882. Governor O. M. Roberts, shown in this picture, provided a detailed account of the fire which destroyed the building in 1881 in his publication *The Capitols of Texas*. Also shown is Senator Lawrence S. Ross, who was governor when the new Capitol was dedicated in 1888.

(below)
The three-story temporary Capitol stood on the west side of the 1000 block of Congress Avenue from 1882 to 1899. Some of the limestone from the Old Stone Capitol was salvaged for the construction of the temporary Capitol. Notice the horse and buggy tethered in the lower left portion of the picture.

Temporary Capitol and part of the west wing of the present Capitol with horses and wagons in foreground. One of the interesting occurrences in this building is described by Audray Bateman: "The violent events of 1887 caused the arrest of the sergeant-at-arms and the speaker of the house, and 56 members of the Legislature were sued. The trouble began when a San Antonio newsman, H. S. Canfield, was banned by resolution from the table for newsmen. According to the resolution, the reporter had written articles which had reflected on 'the personal appearance, manner and habits of certain individuals of the House.' When Canfield tried to enter the door of the House, he was forcibly detained, and he filed complaint of assault against the sergeant-at-arms and the speaker. The case went all the way to the Supreme Court of Texas, but the House won."

(right)
Temporary Capitol burns. After the new Capitol was completed and put into use, the temporary building was used as the Austin High School, as the location of a book publishing firm, and as a residence. According to Max Bickler, then a young boy working for the publishers: "The fire broke out on the third floor when a stove exploded about 8 A.M. The housewife ran down and asked me to put in the alarm. By the time the trucks — they were horse-drawn vehicles in those days — got there, the third floor was blazing . . . The fire gutted the building."

(below)
Firefighters battle the fire in the temporary Capitol building. Spectators have gathered to witness the fire early on the morning of September 30, 1899. Horse-drawn pumper fire equipment was used. At this time, the present Capitol had been occupied for eleven years.

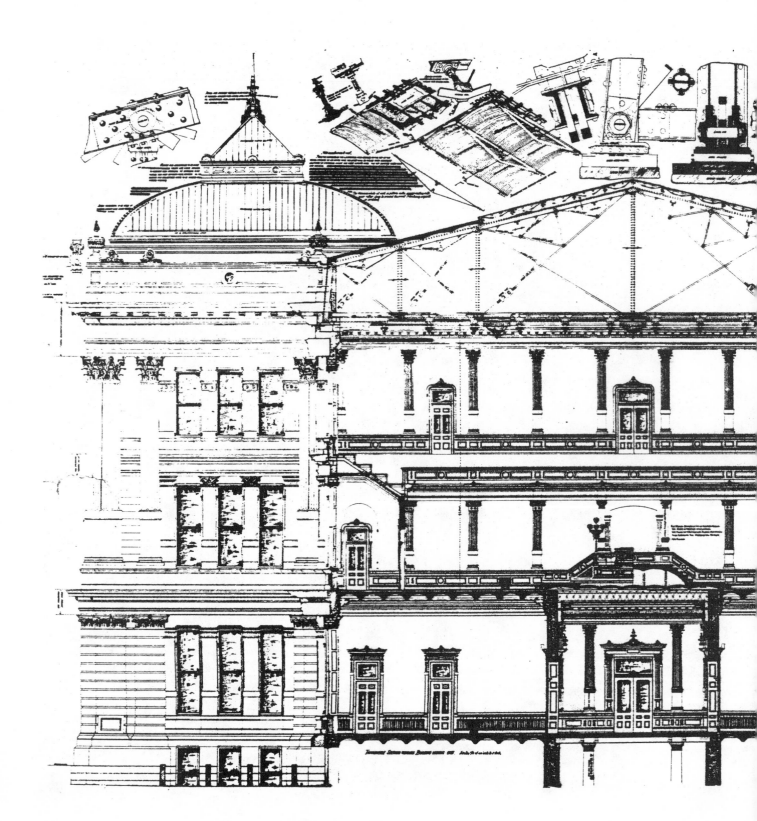

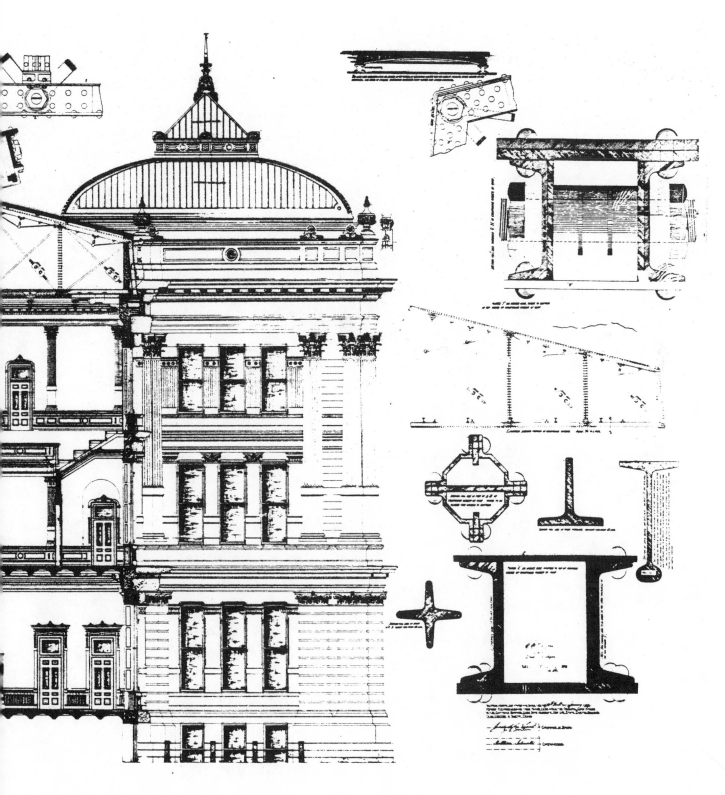

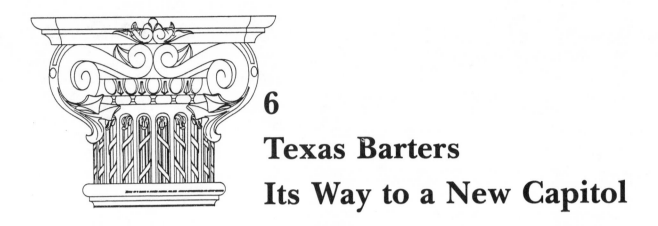

6

Texas Barters
Its Way to a New Capitol

Although the fire that destroyed the Old Stone Capitol provided a dramatic impetus to the need for replacing the statehouse, the idea was already in progress. Texas government had grown rapidly as the population increased, and there were more and more demands for state services. Even the Civil War and the painful era of Reconstruction had not slowed that growth, and it had been apparent for years that a new capitol was inevitable.

Texas, which has had almost as many constitutions as it has had capitals, was ready again to make drastic changes in its rules of law. Although the Constitution of 1869 was only six years old, Texans were ready to abandon it. The document, written by ultra-radicals in the Republican Party, had laid the groundwork for keeping that party in control once Texas was readmitted to the Union after the Civil War. The Convention of 1875 was called primarily to draft a constitution that would allow Democrats to wrest political control from the radical Republicans.

Politics was not the only reason for wanting a new constitution. The state faced many needs not addressed by the 1869 document. An increasing state debt and defense of the frontier were among them. Although it was not high on the agenda, solving the problem of housing the growing government was another.

However, when the delegates met in Austin, one of the first items presented for consideration addressed the need for a new capitol. On November 1, J. R. Fleming of Comanche introduced a resolution requesting the Committee on Public Lands and Land Office "to consider . . . setting apart five million acres of public domain for the purpose of building a State Capitol."

While this was being debated, a substitute was introduced on November 11 that proposed selling only three million acres. Still another proposal would have reduced the acreage to only one million. After careful consideration of each proposal, the committee voted 48 to 14 to recommend that three million acres be earmarked for the building of a new capitol. This action came on November 20, 1875.

Framers of the Constitution of 1876 (which still governs the state) clearly wanted all Texans to have a say in the decision to build a new capitol. They included the proposal as Section 57, Article VI, in the document that went to the voters in February 1876. The proposal was approved by a large majority and became effective the third Tuesday of the following April, but three years passed before the legislature responded to the people's mandate for a new statehouse.

When the 16th Legislature convened in 1879, a bill was introduced providing for the sale of public lands for a new capitol. This made good fiscal sense at the time. The state's treasury was bare, but it still had millions of acres of public lands, much of which was considered worthless. Building a magnificent capitol in exchange for a hunk of desert had to be a good deal for Texas.

Ten Counties for a Capitol

The Act of February 20, 1879, which authorized the sale of the public lands and the start of the new capitol, was a long one. Among other things, it appropriated as the specific acreage to be sold the Panhandle counties of Bailey, Castro, Cochran, Dallam, Deaf Smith, Hartley, Hockley, Lamb, Oldham, and Parmer. It also designated the governor, comptroller, treasurer, attorney general, and land commissioner as a Capitol Board to select a surveyor and oversee the construction to its conclusion. In addition to authorizing these officials to sell the three million acres at no less than fifty cents each, the board approved the sale of another 50,000 to pay for the necessary survey. Indians were still a potential problem at the time, so the act also authorized the governor to provide protection for the surveyor on the frontier.

J. T. Munson of Denison received the surveying contract when the lowest bidder failed to make bond. Munson agreed to do the job for $7,440. The highest bidder had asked $37,900. The contract called for the survey to be completed by September 1, 1880. Munson missed the deadline by only eight days, turning in his field notes and maps on September 8. The General Land Office approved the survey on November 16, 1880, and the first step toward building a new capitol had been made.

It had been five years since the constitutional provision calling for a new capitol had been approved by the people. Now the 16th Legislature moved quickly. Anticipating that Munson's survey would be completed on schedule, the lawmakers wanted to be ready for the next step. On April 18, 1879, they passed an act providing for the building of a new capitol. Joseph Lee of Austin and N. L. Norton of Salado were named as a commission to direct the work under the aegis of the official Capitol Board. J. N. Preston of Austin was chosen as the building superintendent.

Since members of the Capitol Board were all elected officials, turnover was constant. Governors O. M. Roberts, John Ireland, and Lawrence Sullivan Ross served, as did four attorneys general—George McCormick, J. H. McLeary, John D. Templeton, and James Stephen Hogg. So did four comptrollers—Stephen H. Darden, W. M. Brown, W. J. Swain, and John D. McCall—and two land commissioners, W. C. Walsh and R. M. Hall. Only one member of the Capitol Board, State Treasurer F. R. Lubbock, stayed with the project from beginning to end.

A Bargain—Or Was It?

With the Capitol Board and commission in place and a superintendent employed, the state, cash-poor and land-rich, was now ready to find a contractor willing to swap his talents, materials, and labor force for a sizeable and "worthless" slab of Texas. The decision to trade land for an ornate capitol seemed a wise one at the time. Only the hindsight of a century later raises the question of whether the bartering of the acreage was fiscally sound. In 1880 the land traded may have been worth only fifty cents an acre, as determined by appraisers at that time, but by 1988 the same land was valued in the billions of dollars.

The question of whether the trade-off was wise or wasteful remains arguable. But it did give rise to another Texas "brag." Texans today can claim that they have the most expensive capitol ever built by any government anywhere in the world!

1896 XIT photograph of cattle in the sod house pasture in Lamb County. The XIT Ranch first introduced Angus cattle into its herds in 1889. At one time, the XIT was the world's largest ranch. The Capitol Syndicate established this ranch in 1885 with a land trade of three million acres in exchange for the construction of the State Capitol with an additional 50,000-acre survey fee. The XIT Ranch was surrounded by 6,000 miles of barbed wire fence and, at one time, had 150,000 head of cattle. *(Photo courtesy Panhandle-Plains Museum)*

Round-up on the Buck Horn Ranch. Buck Tanner, wagon boss, and other XIT cowboys with their horses pose in front of an XIT chuckwagon. *(Photo courtesy Panhandle-Plains Museum)*

Branding at the Middle Whitely Yellowhouse Division of the XIT Ranch in the early 1890s. *(Photo courtesy Panhandle-Plains Museum)*

7

The Carpenter Who Built a Statehouse

Elijah E. Myers went to college to study law, discovered that he liked carpentry better, and eventually became an architect. One of his notable accomplishments would be the Texas State Capitol.

Finding an architect early was vital. Certainly, the Capitol Board was lacking in any expertise. Land Commissioner W. C. Walsh, in his memoirs of the events leading to the planning of the Capitol, said that only one member of the board had any knowledge of either architecture or construction. He recalled that when the group met the first time, each was asked what experience in building, if any, he had. Governor Oran Roberts, later to be remembered as the beloved "Old Alcalde" by his law students at The University of Texas, replied that he had once built a chimney for a log cabin and daubed it with mud. Another said that he had quarried some building stone and had bossed the job of erecting a two-story house in Austin. The remaining members pleaded "not guilty," Walsh wrote. State Treasurer Francis R. Lubbock was apparently among the latter.

This is surprising since Lubbock, himself a former governor, had built the first executive mansion for the president of the Republic of Texas. He had been in the process of putting up a warehouse in Houston for his business when that village was chosen as the capital. Lubbock made some changes in the unfinished structure, added a second floor and windows, and it became the home of President Sam Houston.

The members' lack of construction experience did not slow action by the board. While waiting for the sale of the 50,000 acres that would finance the survey of the Panhandle lands, the board began its search for an architect. Advertisements in several northern newspapers invited competitive bidding for a plan and specifications for a capitol. The ad listed in general terms the prospective uses and stated that unlimited quantities of native limestone were available.

Eight architects responded, submitting eleven designs. Four of the bidders lived in Texas, but such residence was not a requirement for the job. Of the eight, the only one whose work had received any national attention was Elijah Myers, a Philadelphia native. He had designed the capitol of Michigan in East Lansing and was practicing in Detroit when he read the notice that Texas was soliciting plans for its statehouse.

Once the competitors had submitted their designs, Walsh wrote that the board realized "that we were in water away over our heads."

The members solicited help from Roger Q. Mills, a hero of the Confederacy and at that time a U.S. congressman from Texas. Mills, after eight years in the House, had become one of the most prominent members of Congress and had contacts throughout the country. On his advice, the board asked Napoleon Le Brun, a famed French architect practicing in New York, to act as its advisor in the search.

Le Brun's services weren't cheap. He demanded $3,000 and travel expenses to come to Austin for a period not to exceed three weeks. Governor Roberts and his colleagues agreed that Le Brun's counsel was worth the added cost.

The board, with what Walsh described as "plain common sense," already had rejected four of the plans "and looked askance at a fifth." After carefully reviewing those remaining, Le Brun recommended that the one submitted by Myers be chosen.

Le Brun sent Myers's plan to Governor Roberts with the notation that he thought it combined "in the most convenient and appropriate manner, all of the accommodations needed" in the proposed building. He praised the style of architecture as "simple, harmonious and dignified. The proposed construction is good and [the] manner of lighting, heating and ventilating is as effective as possible in a building of such great magnitude and complex arrangements."

However, Le Brun also had some ideas of his own and presented them to Myers. Although he was never one to accept even constructive criticism lightly, Myers did agree to the modifications. The board also suggested some changes that were made, and on May 17, 1881, Myers signed on as the designing architect. His fee was $12,000.

Myers promised completed plans within six weeks, a deadline which nobody thought he could meet. He didn't. It was October before he completed and sent to the commissioners his first detailed drawings, full specifications, and a form of contract for the builders. Also, J. N. Preston, who had been appointed to work with the commission as superintendent of the project, had resigned and a successor had not been found.

Not all of the bottlenecks that followed were the fault of Myers. For example, his plans had to be copied twice — once for the commissioners and once for the future building contractor. Making such copies was no easy task in the days before machines made this work fast and inexpensive.

Involved were thirty-nine tracings, each four by eight feet. Myers had hoped to reproduce them by a process known as "sun printing," not unlike today's blueprints. However, making such prints required glass of uniform quality, which was not available in Austin. Also, the plans had to be executed in a variety of colors that indicated the different materials used in construction (to help workers who were illiterate or couldn't read English). Unfortunately, sun prints could not reproduce in color.

Thus it was necessary to have expert draftsmen copy and color the plans by hand, a tedious and expensive job. As a result, the final set was not ready until February 1883, some twenty-two months after Myers had accepted the job as architect.

Although Myers was only partly to blame for the delays with the plans, many other problems would follow. His failure to deliver on schedule planted the first seeds of suspicion in the minds of the commissioners that the choice of an architect might have been unwise. The confirmation that Myers may have been a better carpenter than he was an architect would not come until later.

Two Capitols to Replace One

Despite the delays, the Capitol Board had not waited. Their advertisement on July 1, 1881, invited contractors to submit bids "for supplying all materials and completing every class of work required in the construction of a new State Capitol in Austin, Texas." All bids were to be opened on November 15 at noon.

Six days before the scheduled bid opening, however, the Capitol Board and its commissioners were handed a problem far more serious than Myers's tardiness. The existing Capitol burned to the ground on November 9, 1881.

Immediately there were stories that an arsonist had caused the blaze. Rumor had it that it was the work of some cowboys hired by a speculator who had forged some claims to 20,000 acres of land. Fearful that his ruse would be discovered, he decided to torch the statehouse where he believed the records were stored. (Actually, all such records were secure in the fireproof General Land Office building.)

The arson theory was discarded almost immediately by Governor Roberts. It seems that he and two other members of the Capitol Board were meeting to discuss the proposed new statehouse when the fire started in an adjoining room. The fire apparently resulted from a clerk's carelessness and the ignorance of a mechanic. The mechanic had run a stovepipe against the paper and plank side of the room instead of into the flue. The room was full of books and papers, and when a clerk lighted a fire in the woodstove, the conflagration began. Since the old building was little more than kindling wood on the interior and since the water supply was inadequate, the place was doomed. In a few minutes, the Capitol that had been Texas's seat of government for twenty-eight years was destroyed.

Although Austin residents had earlier expressed pride in the state's first permanent capitol, its loss by fire did not sadden them. The knoll it occupied at the head of Congress Avenue, known locally as "Kissing Hill" because it was a favorite spot for courting couples to park their buggies, had developed a somewhat unsavory reputation in some quarters.

Texas Siftings, a weekly humor magazine published in Austin at the time, reported the fire in its November 12 issue this way:

The architectural monstrosity that so long has disfigured the crown of heaven — "Kissing Hill" — at the head of Congress Avenue is no more. Gone is the venerable building that bore such a startling resemblance to a large corn crib with a pumpkin for a dome. No more will its halls respond with legislative eloquence, reminding the distant hearer of a dog barking up a hollow tree.

While the building may have been regarded by some as an eyesore, the destruction of its contents was another matter. Many records dating back to the beginning of the Republic of Texas were lost forever. To Governor Roberts, "the greatest loss was that of the State Library and the collection of geological specimens in the building."

Certainly, the contents of the State Library were irreplaceable. As one of the first agencies established by the Third Congress of the Republic of Texas, the State Library contained thousands of volumes that had been chosen especially by experts like Ashbel Smith. Hundreds of maps, many dating to early Spanish exploration, went up in smoke.

The incident delayed the taking of bids on the new Capitol from November 15, the date originally advertised, until the following January 1, 1882. It also left the state without a place in which to conduct governmental affairs. Immediate steps were taken, however, to solve this problem.

Regardless of what *Texas Siftings* may have said about the histrionics of the legislature, the lawmakers set a new priority to provide a forum where they could give attention, vocal and otherwise, to the state's business. That meant erecting a building in which to work, and they appropriated $45,000 for the construction of a temporary capitol. It was to be located south of the twenty-five acres reserved for the new statehouse and was to be completed and ready for occupancy by January 1, 1883.

Work on the new building proceeded on schedule. By September 1, 1882, the walls had been completed. However, the roof was still missing when a severe rainstorm hit during the night. Water poured into the unprotected building, and by 6:00 A.M., the entire northwestern wing collapsed. The planking that was to receive a tin roof was only partially in place, and it allowed the immense volume of water to stream in on the walls. A reporter for the *Austin Statesman* described the sound of the falling walls as "equal almost to a South American earthquake."

Architects were called in immediately to survey the damage, and their report was disheartening. They recommended that the future safety of the building demanded that the remaining parts of the north and west walls be dismantled and the foundation enlarged. The contractor, necessarily worried about his agreement which limited construction costs, refused to comply. He argued that the expense would be prohibitive. Instead, he agreed only to put iron girders in each of the walls, and this seemed to be enough to assure the state that the building would then be strong and safe.

But the public did not share this confidence. The *Statesman* warned editorially that "it will never be more than a cheap affair." The supreme insult to the temporary capitol came during the following March, when a group of legislators gathered across Congress Avenue in the midst of a windstorm. They had come to watch the building blow down.

The capitol survived, however, and remained in service until the permanent capitol was a reality.

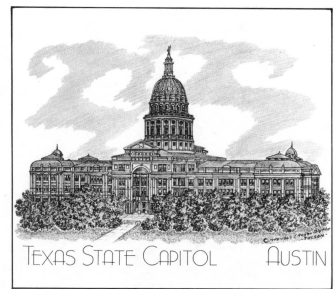

TEXAS STATE CAPITOL   AUSTIN

Elijah E. Myers (1832–1909) became one of the most noted architects of our country. Among the hundreds of buildings designed by Myers, the following state capitol buildings of Michigan, Colorado, and Texas are outstanding.

COLORADO STATE CAPITOL   DENVER

Of the state capitols designed by Elijah E. Myers, Texas is by far the most magnificent of these and the only one to have a double dome.

(Illustrations courtesy of Mrs. T. Roger Blythe)

MICHIGAN STATE CAPITOL LANSING

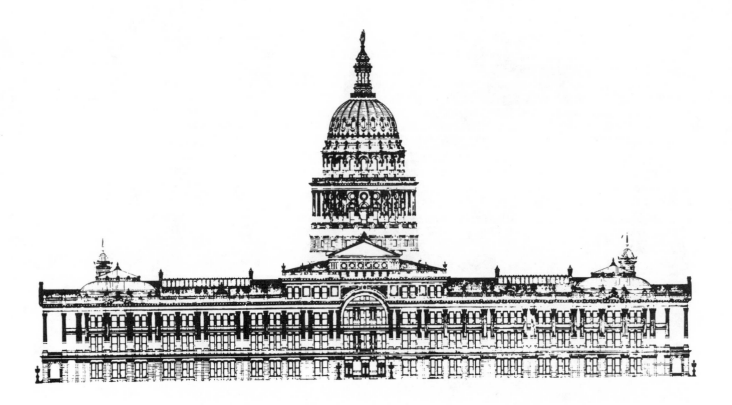

(above)

South elevation of the statehouse from architectural drawings by E. E. Myers. Some of the major dates in the planning, construction, and dedication of the Texas State Capitol are:

20 November 1875 — State Constitution Convention adopts provision by a vote of 48–14 to reserve 3,000,000 acres of land for the purpose of building a state Capitol. Another 50,000 acres was eventually used to pay for the survey of the land.

18 January 1876 — Constitution embodying this provision adopted by the people of Texas.

14 June 1879 — Mr. J. T. Munson awarded contract to survey lands to be sold to finance Capitol.

1 January 1882 — Charles B. and John V. Farwell, brothers from Chicago, agree to build the Capitol and accept as payment 3,000,000 acres of land.

1 February 1882 — Ground Breaking Ceremony, Commissioners Lee and Norton present.

20 February 1882 — Actual excavation of the Capitol began.

30 April 1884 — Report on the quality of limestone submitted by General R. L. Walker, Building Supervisor.

8 December 1884 — General Walker recommended the exterior be changed from limestone to granite.

3 February 1885 — Modified plans to change to granite submitted by E. E. Myers, Capitol Architect.

5 January 1886 — Construction resumed in granite.

October 1886 — Second floor walls neared completion.

13 January 1887 — 14-ounce copper roofing substituted for slate roof.

August 1887 — Dome started.

January 1888 — Roof of the Capitol completed.

26 February 1888 — Goddess of Liberty placed on top of dome.

20 April 1888 — Electricity first turned on in the Capitol.

21 April 1888 — Capitol first opened to the public.

4 May 1888 — Capitol construction report accepted.

8 May 1888 — Preliminary acceptance of Capitol Building.

18 May 1888 — Dedication speech by Senator Temple Houston.

September 1888 — Occupied by Government.

8 December 1888 — Final acceptance of the Capitol by the Capitol Receiving Board.

(rhp)

Double or suspended dome architectural drawing by E. E. Myers. Myers's work was originally submitted under the pseudonym of "Tuebor" and was selected by Napoleon Le Brun of New York over ten other plans. Le Brun's recommendations included a list of suggested modifications and Myers's design was conditionally accepted. In 1881, Myers was paid $12,000 to produce a complete set and two copies of working drawings and specifications. These thirty-nine detailed plans were each approximately four feet by eight feet. These copies were not finished until February 1883.

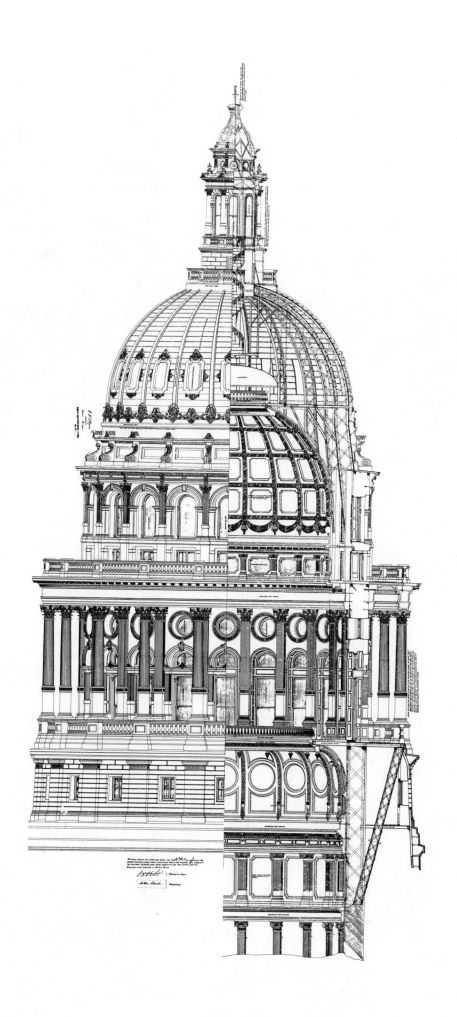

45

(above)

1884 photograph of the Capitol Building site. The four rounded, landscaped areas were part of the landscaping for the Colonial Capitol. In the background is the Old Main Building of The University of Texas, also under construction at the time. The limestone used in the foundation and inner walls of the Capitol was quarried at Oatmanville (Convict Hill) by prison labor. It is believed that eight convicts died there; three were killed attempting to escape and five died from disease or abuse.

(below)

First-floor plan of the Capitol illustrating the "Greek Cross" architectural style. Two long hallways lie east and west and two shorter hallways lie north and south, centered around a rotunda. The darkened areas of this architectural drawing indicate the areas that were originally floored with decorative encaustic tile. The octagon-shaped area of the rotunda was originally covered with glass block tile, which was held in place by metal framing.

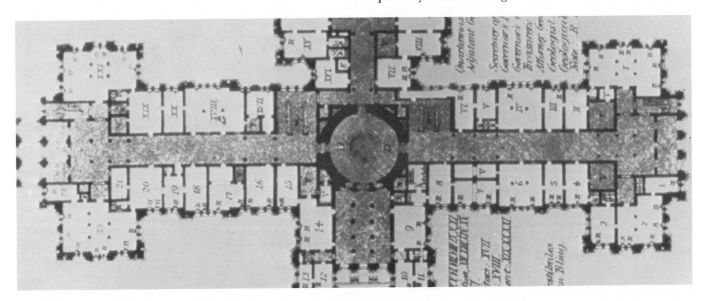

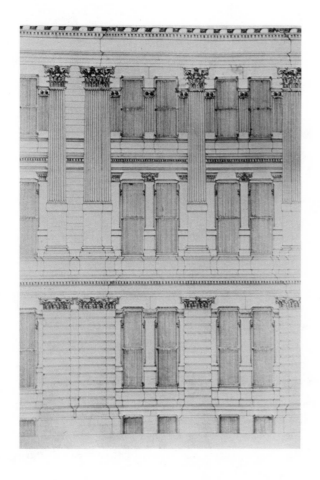

(ul)
Detailed original architectural drawings of the exterior columns, stonework, and windows on the Capitol Building. Much of the Texas State Capitol was modeled after the nation's Capitol.

(ur)
Architectural drawings of the skylight for the north side of the Capitol. On the fifth level of the north wing was a structure with a glass-roofed skylight on top and twenty-four circular cobalt blue with cut design windows on the sides. This filtered an even, blue-tinted north light through acid-etched panels on the ceiling of the fourth level all the way down to the second-floor State Library. An ornate railed opening was on the third floor. The second-level State Library had a glass floor under this beautiful and functional opening.

(ll)
Architect's rendering of one of the doors of the Capitol Building. Each door was made up of beautiful wood carvings and acid-etched glass in the door panels and transoms. The transom glass usually named the arm of government housed in that area. In 1888 there were 404 doors in the completed building.

8

The Contract
Is Let

Bids for the construction of the permanent capitol were opened on January 1, 1882. There were only two bidders, but it was almost miraculous that there were any at all under the terms that Texas demanded. The contractor was to receive no cash, which meant that he had to finance the project from his own resources. The only payment to him would be the three million acres of land, which even the state considered to be of little worth.

Texas owned more than 48 million acres at the time, but the area selected as barter for its new capitol included some of the least valuable. Located on the so-called High Plains, it had neither trees nor hills to break the desertlike expanse. Only the lazy Canadian River and a few dry creeks watered the area. Experts doubted that there were underground reservoirs that could be tapped.

In 1876, when the legislature created the fifty-four Panhandle counties, the land was considered a part of the Great American Desert and was generally believed to be too arid for settlement. A few pioneers had risked homesteading in the area, but their numbers remained few. Thus it appeared that Texas was trading wasteland for its new capitol, and most contractors weren't interested.

The two bidders were A. A. Burck of Rockdale and Mattheas Schnell of Rock Island, Illinois. Burck's bid was the lowest, but only if the board consented to some changes in the plans. On this basis, Schnell's bid, although higher, was clearly the best deal. When Schnell posted the required $250,000 performance bond, his bid was accepted.

Because Schnell was given the contract, it was assumed by the Capitol Commission that he would do the work. As events developed, however, his actual role in the construction was insignificant. The ink was hardly dry on the contract before he asked that three-fourths of his interest be assigned to a Chicago firm known as Taylor, Babcock, and Co.

The firm, to be called the Capitol Syndicate while executing the contract, had four principals: brothers Charles B. and John V. Farwell, Abner Taylor, and Amos C. Babcock. Taylor, a member of Congress from Illinois, was the only bona fide builder, having been the principal contractor in the rebuilding of Chicago after the tragic fire there. Charles Farwell was the U.S. senator from Illinois; Babcock was interested in a behind-the-scenes role in politics, and was a friend and supporter of both the senator and congressman; and John Farwell owned a large merchandising business in Chicago.

Senator Farwell, who hoped to be president of the United States, had helped to organize the Republican party in Illinois. He also had sponsored Lincoln for president and was considered a likely possibility himself to occupy the White House. John Farwell, a crafty dry goods merchant, believed that the Texas land could become an unlimited financial resource in time.

Congressman Taylor, like Senator Farwell, saw the capitol project as a possible way to finance his own political future. Taylor and Babcock were long-time friends who had soldiered together in the Union Army and later had become partners in a couple of business ventures without much success. Although Taylor had been the major contractor who had profited from the Chicago conflagration, he was not a financial success, having allowed his dabbling in politics to interfere with his business. As a result, he had never acquired much money.

Babcock had even less of the world's goods, although many considered him a creative genius. After the Chicago fire he had patented a new kind of fire extinguisher, but it, and some of his other inventions, never caught on. He devoted most of his energy to the political scene and had worked with the Farwells and Taylor in organization of the Republican party in Illinois.

Thus a combination of circumstances drew the quartet together on the Texas project and resulted in the formation of the Capitol Syndicate. The Farwells furnished the money, Taylor was responsible for the actual construction, and Babcock was a sort of free-floating ombudsman. Senator Farwell looked after their interests in Washington, but brother John left his wholesale operations to manage the work on the Capitol. He had the last word on all decisions.

John Farwell's other assignment from the syndicate was to get some revenue coming in from the land for which they had bartered their services and investment in materials. None of the four had any experience in ranching, yet they decided to turn their three million acres into a ranch three times larger than any that exists today. As soon as title to the land was transferred to the syndicate's name in July 1885, Farwell hired Ab Blocker, a veteran traildriver, to deliver the first cattle.

It was Blocker who created the XIT brand — one that was to make the ranch famous around the world. In his hurry to get the new cattle marked, he dragged the letters XIT in the dust with the heel of his boot and suggested that this be the brand. At the ranch's peak, 150,000 head of cattle would wear XIT on their hides as they roamed an area almost 200 miles long and averaging 27 miles in width. Almost 6,000 miles of barbed wire — twice the distance between New York and Los Angeles — was required just to fence it.

The syndicate partners never intended to make ranching a lifelong work. Their first interest was in making money, and their long-range hope was that the land later could be converted to agriculture. Eventually, they planned to subdivide it and sell it in small parcels and, perhaps, even create towns and cities.

Stocking the ranch with its first cattle cost more money than the syndicate could raise, so it formed a land and investment company in London and sold bonds to the English. Although Farwell saw to it that the XIT had good management and that Hereford, Shorthorn, and Angus cattle were introduced to upgrade and replace the original Texas breeds, the ranch operated in the red. To avoid bankruptcy, the syndicate began selling off the land wholesale in 1901. That year, it sold 500,000 acres for $1 million.

Such was the beginning of the end of the XIT as a ranch. By 1912, it was no longer in the cattle business. By 1950, the heirs of the original syndicate owners had sold all but 20,000 acres.

In more than a half century, the three million acres of "worthless" land turned out to be one of the most profitable payments to a building contractor ever. The builders of the Capitol eventually spent $3.7 million on the project and the state of Texas another $520,000 above the value of the land. Today, however, the acreage Texas traded for the building is busy producing a variety of crops as well as oil and is valued for tax purposes at almost $7 *billion*.

On that basis, the red granite Capitol in Austin is the most expensive government building ever erected anywhere in the world.

9

The Construction Begins

While John Farwell was getting the XIT Ranch started and his brother was taking care of his Illinois constituents, Abner Taylor, as the syndicate's designated builder, was on the job in Austin. He wanted to get work on the new capitol started as quickly as possible so he and his colleagues could take title to their promised lands.

The contract called for construction to start on February 1, 1882. Taylor saw to it that ground was broken that day.

Groundbreaking was not an auspicious occasion. Only a small crowd of citizens came out for the ceremony, including Commissioners Joseph Lee and N. L. Norton. No members of the Capitol Board were present and no other state official attended. Under other circumstances, these absences might have been disconcerting to Taylor, but he was too concerned over other problems to be bothered by the lack of pomp and circumstance at turning the first dirt.

To begin with, he estimated that it would take twelve months to prepare the foundation. The Capitol Board insisted that this time be shortened. However, because the board also required the use of all native materials, Taylor had to build a railroad from the limestone quarry west of Austin, a distance of some nine miles. He then had to run a spur line from the International & Great Northern Railroad depot at Third and Congress to get the stone to the Capitol site.

To save time and money, Taylor planned to build the spur from the station up the center of Congress Avenue. The Austin City Council vetoed that idea. After much haggling, he was allowed to run his rails north up East Avenue, then west on Eleventh Street to Capitol Hill. It was March 1884 before he got the rails in place.

The rail lines were but one of many problems that were to plague the construction of the Capitol from start to finish. Taylor was still excavating and working on the foundation in 1883 when what purported to be the "final" drawings arrived from Myers, the architect, who was doing the work in his Detroit office. They were so full of errors and discrepancies that Taylor sent them back with word that Myers had only until January 1, 1884, to correct them. Myers, responding that he was ill, would not arrive in Austin until January 18.

By then, the legislature was in session and members of the Capitol Board and commission were too busy to see him. He returned to Detroit in a huff, leaving most of the problems unsolved and questions unanswered.

Myers's apparent indifference to the project angered the board. At one point, it ordered Attorney General John D. Templeton "to place the bond . . . of Myers in suit at once." The matter never got to court, but Myers was directed to come to Austin a second time in June 1885. He claimed illness again, but finally arrived on October 8. His stay was brief and he failed to make the modifications Taylor had requested. After returning to Detroit, he promised to come back to Austin on January 1, 1886.

Once again in Michigan, however, he entered a disclaimer to the allegations of the Texas attorney general. He claimed that "the plans and specifications are in no respect defective or insufficient." Myers failed to return to Austin as promised, finally resigned from the project, and suffered a mental breakdown.

His illness, however, is not the reason that even today the Capitol remains unfinished. The original plans called for each of the side entrances to have two-storied, columned porticoes, but these were never built because the Capitol Board discovered that the project was over-budget.

Why the Capitol Got a Pink Face

Despite the architect's recalcitrance in correcting the plans, workmen at the Oatmanville quarry (now the Austin suburb of Oak Hill) were busy. At a cost of $100,000, several huge boulders had been quarried and dressed. To handle the stones, nine heavy derricks were at the quarry and ten at the building site. Each could lift eight to ten tons of stone. On March 4, 1884, the first sixty tons came steaming down Eleventh Street on the new railroad.

Lee and Norton, the two commissioners, took one look and rejected the limestone. The stone was found to contain iron pyrites, which caused it to discolor when exposed to the weather. This bit of intelligence should have come as no surprise to the commission or the contractor. They had failed to listen to the man they had appointed superintendent of construction — Gen. R. L. Walker of Richmond, Virginia.

J. N. Preston, the first superintendent, had resigned in 1881 before the building contract was even awarded. He was succeeded by W. D. Clark, who stayed through the end of 1883. Walker had only taken the job in February 1884 but had reported almost at once that the Oatmanville limestone was unstable. He warned that once exposed to wind, rain, and sun, the stone would be marked by dirty, rusty streaks. He predicted that if native limestone was used on the exterior, the Texas Capitol, planned as a glorious white, would be gray streaked with orange as it aged.

Contractor Taylor agreed and offered a solution. A quarry in Bedford, Indiana, produced exactly the type of limestone needed. He was familiar with the product and knew that it met all specifications. But this was not to be.

John Ireland had succeeded Oran Roberts in 1883 as governor, and he vetoed any use of the Hoosier product. Ireland already was unhappy because the architect, the contractor, and many of the workmen were not Texans. He insisted that the materials, at least, had to be native to the state.

Fortunately for the looks of the future Capitol, limestone was not the only building material available among the many resources of Texas.

A Saddle Horse for a Granite Mountain

Near Marble Falls, seventy-five railroad miles from Austin, there was a ranch with a small mountain of solid granite which occupied one entire section (640 acres). It was operated by G. W. Lacy, who also had two partners — W. H. Westfall and N. L. Norton. To the owners, and particularly to Lacy, the hard rock in the middle of their ranch was useless. They couldn't run a single cow on Granite Mountain.

This barrier to his cattle business had worried Lacy for years. On one occasion, he had offered to trade the entire mountain to a neighbor in exchange for a good saddle horse. The neighbor, recognizing a bad bargain when he saw one, simply smiled and shook his head "no."

When Lacy and his partners heard about the decision to abandon the Oatmanville limestone as the Capitol exterior, however, they saw a way out of their dilemma. Pink granite was more durable than limestone, and it would be the perfect material for the new building. In a magnanimous gesture, the owners decided to present to the state as much granite from their mountain as needed for the new Capitol. Since one of the owners, Norton, was a commissioner supervising the project, this seemed to be an especially public-spirited gesture.

Texans had become aware that native granite might be the new material, but many still wanted limestone. They hoped that the new statehouse would look like a replica of the national Capitol in Washington. By the time the cornerstone was laid on March 3, 1885, however, the excitement was such that nobody seemed to care any longer which material would provide the building's exterior.

Photograph of basement-level construction of the Capitol late in 1882. These first walls were of limestone. The *Daily Statesman* of February 2, 1882, tells of the original groundbreaking: "Contract for the new state house required that work should begin on the first day of February, and yesterday that contract was fully complied with . . . Colonel N. L. Norton and Judge Joseph Lee, commissioners, shoveled the first dirt, and Captain [Ed] Creary and Mr. John P. Kirk followed with their spades and thus began the work of the great edifice, which is to require six long years to build. There were a number of citizens present, but none of the government officials. Messrs. Creary and Haswell will have a force of hands to work in earnest tomorrow.

. . . The new capitol will front about one hundred and thirty feet in rear of the north or rear wall of the old state house and will reach some distance into the street on the north . . . The people of Austin may expect lively times when the work gets fairly underway.

. . . Mr. John P. Kirk, who handled the third shovel full of dirt yesterday on the new Capitol work, took out the second shovel of dirt from the excavation at the old Capitol over thirty years ago. He was a small boy at the time, and placed one of his glass playing marbles in the cornerstone at the building. He proposes to have that same marble placed in the cornerstone of the new edifice."

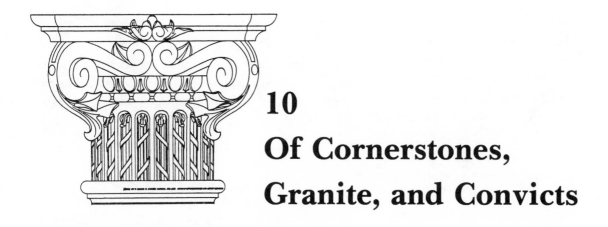

10

Of Cornerstones, Granite, and Convicts

Unlike the ceremonies of July 3, 1852, when the cornerstone for the first permanent capitol was laid in Austin, the second occasion attracted a large crowd. As one writer described it: "Everyone of any distinction was present, and just about everyone of no distinction also was there."

The man behind the occasion was Gus Wilke of Chicago. He had been the subcontractor on the Capitol foundation and basement and had developed a personal interest in the project. Wilke wanted the cornerstone ceremony to be memorable and went to considerable trouble and expense to make it so. He selected as the date for the occasion March 2, 1883 — the forty-ninth anniversary of Texas's declaration of independence from Mexico. And since it was almost certain that granite would be the building's exterior, Wilke wanted the cornerstone to come from Granite Mountain.

No railroad existed from Marble Falls, so Wilke arranged to have the 18,000-pound stone cut and hauled fifteen miles to the Burnet railhead by ox team. From there it traveled to Austin by train. Wilke paid for the quarrying, cutting, transportation, dressing, polishing, and engraving himself — a total of $1,545.

Land Commissioner W. C. Walsh represented the Capitol Board and presided at the ceremony. A prayer by the Reverend Homer S. Thrall of San Antonio began the event. Governor Ireland delivered the main speech, followed by Judge George Quinan of Wharton County.

Members of the Grand Lodge of Texas, Ancient Free and Accepted Masons, were given the honor of placing the stone. Col. Frank B. Sexton spoke for them. He was introduced by A. P. Wooldrige, Austin banker and civic leader. The ceremony ended with the Travis Light Artillery firing a forty-nine-gun sa-

lute, followed by a benediction from the Reverend J. W. Whipple of Austin.

The cornerstone graces the northeast corner of the Capitol. In the process of being cut, dressed, polished, and engraved, the stone lost 6,000 pounds of its weight. As set, it weighs not quite six tons. It measures four feet ten inches by four feet ten inches by ten feet eight inches. For a building that was one of the world's largest at the time it was completed, the cornerstone is small.

Like all such markers, it houses mementoes of varying historical significance. Francis R. Lubbock, in his role as state treasurer, was given the responsibility to select items for inclusion. A stone from the earlier capitol; currency of the Republic of Texas, and of the Confederate States of America; an Austin city directory; and an 1862 meal ticket worth twenty-five cents are among the objects preserved. So is the gavel used in the cornerstone-laying ceremony. These and similar artifacts were placed in a zinc box, which rests in a space hollowed out of the center of the granite base.

The inscription on the stone is brief. On the east side are the dates "March 2, 1836 — March 2, 1885" with the state seal carved between them. Around the seal are the words "The State of Texas." On the north side is the legend "Commenced February 1, 1881," the date when construction actually began.

Why Not Granite and Limestone, Too?

With the cornerstone in place, a decision as to which stone to use in the building had to be made. The owners of Granite Mountain had told the state of their intentions to donate the stone needed for the project but had not yet come forward with a formal offer. Taylor, the contractor, still opted for Indiana limestone, but he couldn't void the contract that specified native Texas material.

However, Taylor had the support of the Capitol Commission in behalf of the Hoosier stone. The commissioners wanted construction to get on as quickly as possible, as did the syndicate. Taylor, aware of the deficiencies of the Oatmanville limestone, also was convinced that the quarry simply wasn't large enough to produce enough material to finish the building, even if the quality of the stone was acceptable. The commission agreed and informed Governor Ireland that the Indiana material should be accepted.

Ireland refused to be swayed. More than any other individual, the governor was responsible for the eventual choice of granite. Public opinion had also shifted, and the majority of the voters also wanted the Texas stone. To get it, Ireland was quite willing to play a waiting game with the contracting syndicate and to delay the construction, if necessary.

The governor knew he held the winning hand because time was on his side. The businessmen who had taken on the contract wanted to show a profit for their investors from the ranching operations they were developing on the West Texas land. Such a profit became less and less likely as work was delayed and building costs increased. It was to their advantage to complete the building as quickly as possible.

Taylor was very much aware of this, and his only real objection to granite was cost. If the stone had to be purchased, he figured the additional out-of-pocket expense to the syndicate would be $600,000. It also would be more expensive to haul and dress the stone. However, a few days after the cornerstone was laid, Lacy and his partners informed the Capitol Board that it could have as much stone as it needed from Granite Mountain for free.

This resolved most, but not all, of Taylor's misgivings. He presented this proposal:

> I will construct the building using Texas granite for the exterior wall: provided that the State will furnish me with a granite quarry, and accessible for the building, free of cost, and furnish such number of convicts as I may require, not to exceed 1,000, I to board, clothe and guard them. The enclosed plan of construction be adopted, all the work to be rock faced. The porticoes to be eliminated. Such alterations in the interior as will conform with this plan, not detrimental to the building, and to lessen the cost by $100,000. The time

for completion of the building to be extended three years.

These were exactly the concessions that Governor Ireland and the Capitol Board wanted. They also had the support of General Superintendent Walker. He told the board:

> We are constructing a statehouse for the ages. A Capitol for the greatest state in the Union . . . and what will be the additional expense of a few hundred thousand dollars to such a state, with all the resources of a great empire within itself, when the advantage from that expense will be of benefit to the appearance of the building of which the people of Texas may well be proud, the proportions of which are second only to the National Capitol in magnitude, and far more symmetrical in structure.

The Capitol Board did not react immediately to Taylor's proposal, which was presented on July 16. Work on the Capitol had been at a standstill since May, and the board wanted time to study the contractor's propositions carefully. The board had won its main point—getting a building made of Texas granite. Thus members were agreeable to compromising a bit so the contractors could make their profit, and to making some omissions in the plans to compensate for the additional costs of cutting and preparing the free granite.

The board directed the commissioners to prepare a list of the modifications in the building as Myers had planned it. This resulted in the deletion of the east and west porticoes. In return, the contractor agreed to widen the interior walls and alter the construction of the dome in order to improve the safety of the building.

Men in Stripes: A Unique Crew

The request for the use of convicts from the state prison to quarry the granite required careful study.

Although it was a real problem for the commission and board, Taylor's request for 1,000 prisoners was not a precedent. Gus Wilke had been furnished with convict labor at the Oatmanville quarry while he was doing the foundation work and building the Capitol basement. He had leased 1,000 acres at Oatmanville (Austinites still know the old quarry as "Convict Hill" on the western edge of suburban Oak Hill) and then found labor to dig the limestone both expensive and in short supply. The state had come to Wilke's aid and leased able-bodied convicts from the

Huntsville prison to do the work. On November 18, 1884, the first camp had been started at Oatmanville and eventually 100 prisoners were living under guard in the crude frame buildings. They had done a good job, quarrying up to ten railroad cars of limestone each day by the spring of 1885.

Principal opposition to the use of convict labor on the project had come from the stonecutters' union. Now that Taylor wanted up to 1,000 more prisoners to work at Granite Mountain, the board's problem was magnified. The decision to use granite for the exterior had only exacerbated the situation. Since limestone still would be the interior material, prison labor would have to be used at both quarries.

The board decided that expediency was more important than the objections of the union. On July 21 they voted to give Taylor the convicts that he needed. He would pay the state sixty-five cents a day for their labor and bear the expense of feeding and clothing them. All of Taylor's other proposals were accepted, including a three-year extension on the time to complete the building. The board expressed the hope, however, that the additional months would not be needed.

Meanwhile, Taylor had been having personal problems. After borrowing heavily from Senator Farwell and mortgaging much of his own syndicate stock, he also felt the need to return to Illinois and mend his political fences there. Shortly after he signed the new agreement with the state on July 25, 1885, he sublet the entire contract to Gus Wilke. The commission and board were delighted since Wilke had done an outstanding job as subcontractor on the foundation and basement. Also, his planning and direction of the cornerstone ceremonies had been so successful.

The *Austin American-Statesman* gave Wilke's work a pat on the back some eight months later when it said editorially: "The man who can take a look at the beautiful granite walls of the new Capitol, now going up, and regret that the change was made to that stone, should be kicked out of Texas."

Possibly the most pleased of all with the switch to granite were the donors of the stone. Their gift began the quarrying of granite in Texas. From the 640 acres that couldn't be traded for one saddle horse in 1881 have come millions of tons of stone valued at many more millions of dollars. After the state had taken all of the free granite that it needed for the Capitol construction, Lacy sold the mountain for $90,000 in 1890. In the deal, Lacy not only deeded the mountain and another 2,000 acres, but included the right to quarry granite on 5,000 additional acres.

The quarrying business has since mushroomed in Texas. In the century since the Capitol was built, stone from Granite Mountain and other quarries operating in the area has been used in buildings worldwide. One of the first to be built in Texas after the Capitol was the beautiful Tarrant County Courthouse in Fort Worth.

Today Texas granite is a component of skyscrapers, courthouses, banks, shopping centers, and plazas in cities as diverse as Atlanta, Denver, New York, and Seattle. More than 225,000 tons of the pink rock went into the seven-mile seawall that protects Galveston from the Gulf of Mexico.

(above)

Cornerstone of the Texas State Capitol. On Monday, March 2, 1885, the Texas Capitol cornerstone was laid in place at an elaborate ceremony with approximately 20,000 people in attendance. Some of the words spoken by Rev. Homer S. Thrall that day were: "This house, beautiful for situation, crowning the hill which overlooks our Capitol City, is to be of exceeding magnificence. May it stand for generations and centuries, a center of wholesome political influence and power."

(left)

Invitation to the dedication and laying of the cornerstone on March 2, 1885. The event attracted a large crowd of prideful Texans.

(above)
Oxen and wagon were used to haul the nine-ton cornerstone from the quarry near Marble Falls to Burnet. From Burnet, the specially built railroad took the cornerstone to Austin.

(left)
The cornerstone, weighing approximately 18,000 pounds in the rough and 12,000 pounds finished, was laid in place with mast and boom. Engraving and placing the stone cost approximately $1,545. The cornerstone is on the northeast corner, as are all cornerstones which are correctly placed as prescribed by the Masonic Order. The cornerstone is made of Texas pink granite.

(this page)

Prisoners at work in the granite stone-shaping yard. Much of the work was done with hammers and chisels. Governor Ireland, acting through the Texas Penitentiary Commission, tendered the services of 1,000 convict laborers, free of charge to the contractor, to build a railroad to the quarry and to quarry and dress the stone. As described in the Austin *Statesman* of July 23, 1886: "The convicts are behaving well . . . The quarries seem to be alive with men. Huge stones are piled up in every direction."

(urhp)

Armed prison guards with dogs at Granite Mountain quarry. The April 13, 1886, edition of the Austin *Statesman* reported: "There were about forty guards to supervise the work of three hundred convicts at the granite quarry. There were four cooks, three dishwashers, three laundrymen, several wood-cutters, and about a dozen families who were connected with the work at the quarry . . . The building for the prisoners was enclosed by a wire fence which surrounded a two-acre tract of ground, and the enclosure was patrolled by guards."

(lrhp)

Convicts shaping columns in stoneyards. It is possible that one of these columns might be shown as it is lowered into place in another photo of construction at the Capitol. The flatcars to the right are loaded with granite blocks for shipment to Austin. The convict in the extreme right portion of the photograph makes a universal gesture to the photographer. Temple Houston praised the convict labor in his dedication speech of May 1888: "The services of more than one thousand men were used daily for over four years, and a great part of this time, the work progressed night and day."

58

59

Granite Mountain in Burnet County teems with supervisors and workers. The railroad tracks at right were used for transporting the Texas "sunset red" granite to Austin. It is said that the owner of Granite Mountain, G. W. Lacy, once tried to trade Granite Mountain for a saddle horse. He and his partners were later able to create a quarry business in 1881 by donating the granite for the State Capitol.

Quarrying the granite for the State Capitol. The pulley system used in loading the transport carts shown at the crest of the granite formation is photographed here. Prisoners are at left. In the *Report of Superintendent of Texas Penitentiaries* of October 31, 1886, an analysis of conditions at Granite Mountain was provided: "The discipline at the quarries was good. There was little punishment of the prisoners, and escapes were very few . . . only six escapes occurred during one year of time. The prisoners at Burnet attended church services once per week."

(this page)
The "Lone Star" locomotive engine used to haul 15,700 car-loads of Texas pink granite from Burnet County to Capitol Hill. The narrow gauge railroad was specially built for this purpose. Much of the railroad line that was used to transport this stone was actually built by the convicts. About nine miles of track was constructed from the limestone quarries in Oatmanville to Austin and about sixteen miles of track was laid from Burnet to the Granite Mountain quarries. Track was already in place from Burnet to Austin.

(urhp)
Convicts at work on Granite Mountain. By December of 1885, there were over 300 prisoners quarrying and shaping pieces for the Capitol. This granite became the exterior stone for the Capitol.

(lrhp)
Leased convicts being taken out to the granite quarry to begin work. The shackled prisoners were leased from the prison at a rate of three dollars per month, with food and housing to be furnished by the contractor. These convicts were guarded by armed guards on horseback and by dogs. Legend says that prisoners at Granite Mountain were housed in a large underground tunnel with only one entrance.

64

(ulhp)

Northwestern view of the new Capitol building, showing the original General Land Office Building in the background. The *Austin Daily Statesman* of April 10, 1886 reported: "The man who can take a look at the beautiful granite walls of the new capitol, now going up, and regret that the change was made to that stone, should be kicked out of Texas."

(llhp)

Photograph of construction, taken from a northwestern vantage point in July 1886. The first floor has been completed and work has begun on the second level. Abner Taylor, the contractor, was forced to build a fence around the site to keep spectators out of the way. The derricks with boom and mast could each handle up to ten tons of material. The exterior walls of the Capitol required 15,000 carloads of granite. Twenty of the stones used on the first floor exterior weighed 16,000 pounds each. Notice the advertisements on the fence.

(this page)

Construction of the second floor of the building. This picture was taken from the original Land Office Building on the southeast portion of the Capitol grounds. Work is starting on the third floor, using the masts and booms for placing the enormous granite blocks. Some of the workers lived on the grounds in the construction building shown in front of the Capitol.

65

11

Made in Texas — By Non-Union Labor

The decision to use convict labor on the Capitol would plague the project throughout and continue even after its dedication. The result would be a boycott by the International Association of Granite Cutters Union, a cat-and-mouse game to import illegal stonemasons, and the indictment of the contractor on a criminal charge.

As early as 1884, the national union of granite cutters had started criticizing the Capitol project for the failure of the contractor to employ union labor. The organization became more irate when Taylor, with the state's blessing, brought in convicts to cut limestone at the Austin quarry. When the new contractor, Gus Wilke, elected to increase the number of convict workers, union opposition erupted into action.

The decision to use prisoners was not based on opposition to organized labor. Neither Wilke nor the first contractor, Abner Taylor, were non-union. Both the Capitol Board and the commission had misgivings about using convicts and never planned to do so. But in 1883–85 a depression hit the entire country. The slowing of the economy made it difficult, and later impossible, for the contractors to develop the needed income from the three million acres of land that was to be their only payment. If they had been forced to pay union wages, they would have faced bankruptcy.

Converting the land into a ranch and stocking it with cattle and personnel had proved more expensive than anticipated. As a result, the owners protested their ability to fulfill the Capitol contract. At the same time, both the state and the contractor recognized that neither would win by allowing the syndicate to withdraw from the project and sacrifice the $250,000 cash bond it had posted. Such action would only delay the building and force the state to look for another contractor.

Wilke, when he took over the contract, recognized the problem and tried to avoid it. In August 1884, when he was only the subcontractor working on the foundation, he had run advertisements in national newspapers for thirty experienced stonecutters. He offered union scale wages. The only response from the national union was to run a notice in its journal asking its members "to keep away from Austin State Capitol until further notice."

The union had reasons that it considered valid for its warning. Some convicts already were employed on the project and the national organization did not want its master granite cutters to work alongside these unskilled workers. The convicts might learn the expertise required of the trade, and this eventually might make it difficult for craftsmen to get jobs.

Even the Climate Was a Factor

The Austin local of the union was even more vehement in its opposition. In the national journal, the secretary of the local reported that no union labor had ever been employed on the project. To Wilke's claim in his advertisement that the climate was "good, healthy," the Austin union official warned that the weather in the capital was a foretaste of General Sheridan's description of war.

Wilke knew that he had to find some professional stonemasons, but he was not willing to bow to the demands of the union. The *Austin American-Statesman* reported on December 10, 1885, that the contractor had written the union as follows:

I . . . shall hire any good mechanic whether he be a scab, as you call him, or not. I will not permit you . . . to dictate whom I shall employ, whether they be convicts or free labor. I had experience with enough unions and will not permit them to manage my business . . . I will employ convicts to quarry and dress the stone . . . which will not interfere with the granite cutters . . . that I can see.

The granite cutters' union responded by voting 500 to 1 to boycott the Capitol project.

Meanwhile, union representatives had met with Wilke and he modified his stand somewhat. On December 23, he wired the national headquarters that he would pay skilled union workers $2.75 to $3 a day. Since the prevailing wage in Austin was $4 a day, the union flatly rejected the offer.

The Invasion of Scotland

Although by now Wilke had up to 500 convicts cutting and dressing stone at sixty-five cents a day plus board, he still desperately needed professionals. In the spring of 1886 he sent his personal representative, George Berry, to Scotland with a single duty: to find 150 granite cutters and 15 blacksmiths and tool sharpeners in that country and bring them to America.

On May 2, Berry placed an advertisement for artisans in an Aberdeen newspaper. The offer was considered good for the times. Each would receive $4 a day, guaranteed for eighteen months, but would pay $16 to $20 monthly for room and board. Prospects had to ante up "earnest money" to guarantee that they would come to America. They also would be assessed the cost of their passage to the U.S., which would be paid in two monthly installments.

The ploy was partially successful, and Berry rounded up eighty-six workers and put them on boats for Texas. When Berry and two dozen of the Scots arrived in New York, however, they were met by representatives of the stonecutters' union and a U.S. marshal. Importing foreign labor under contract was a violation of immigration laws, but the federal officer failed to find proof of any such agreement.

Union officials got another story when they interviewed the workers. Each of the new arrivals said that they had a written contract. Charges were then filed against both Berry and his boss, Wilke, and the twenty-four Scots refused to proceed on to Texas.

The other sixty-two workers were on another ship that was to dock in Galveston, but they were not on board when it arrived in the Texas port. Anticipat-

ing possible trouble on landing, they had left the ship at Newport News, Virginia, simply as new immigrants. From there they had taken a train for Austin. This bit of cloak-and-dagger drama had them on the job by May 3. Their services were vital to Wilke if he was to finish the contract by the December 31, 1889, deadline.

Thanks to the Scotch masons (sixty-four eventually were at work), 1886 held the brightest promise of any period since work on the Capitol began. By July, the walls of the first story were completed. The imported experts were hard at work and doing a competent job at both Granite Mountain and the Oatmanville quarry. Wilke was pleased with the progress, but not very happy with his treatment by the U.S. government.

The charges that had been filed against him, Berry, and the syndicate for illegally importing foreign labor were moved to the federal court in Austin. There all were indicted by a grand jury. The Knights of Labor, which had lost its strike against the railroads, voted $5,000 to help defray the government's cost of prosecuting the case. The International Association of Stone Cutters actively urged that the culprits be brought to trial.

The matter dragged on. In August 1887, charges were dropped against the two Farwells and Amos Babcock, but Taylor remained a defendant along with the others. By the time the case went to trial in August 1889, only Wilke remained among those originally charged. He was fined $64,000 — $1,000 for each Scot who remained on the job and another $1,000 in costs. This judgment was not executed until 1893, five years after the Capitol was finished. By then the fine had been reduced to $8,000 and costs.

The verdict did not satisfy the union. Its members felt that Wilke had only been chastised, not punished, for breaking the law. They also were aware that the federal charges had not affected the work on the Capitol and thus had not helped the union's cause. Later, both Wilke and Berry, hoping to improve their relations with the union on future jobs, paid the organization fines of $500.

There Were Italian Masons, Too

In the annals of the building of the Capitol there is little mention of another small group of foreign masons who worked on the project. They were the Italians.

Italians were among the first Europeans to arrive in Texas, although their numbers have never been very large. Amerigo Vespucci, the Italian for whom this continent is named, viewed the Texas coast only five years after Columbus discovered America. There were Italians in Coronado's expedition across the High Plains in 1541.

Apparently, Wilke did not import any Italian artisans when he concentrated his search on Scotland. Some masons from Italy already were living in Texas, and a few helped on the construction of the Capitol.

A Top-Heavy Capitol

By the late summer of 1887, Wilke's work force—now totaling 900— had all but completed the exterior of the main floors, including the ornamentation. New problems awaited them, however, as they began constructing the dome.

Myers, the architect, had called for capping the building with a dome of brick. It was to be five feet thick at the base, diminishing gradually in thickness to the foot of the lantern. The dome would tower 100 feet and be the finishing adornment for what Myers envisioned as the gem of state capitols.

Fortunately, however, Land Commissioner Walsh was also something of an amateur architect. As a member of the Capitol Board from its inception, he had studied each detail of construction as the building progressed. And he was worried about Myers's plan for the dome.

Walsh began by figuring the total weight of the brick to be used and then adding the weight of the substructure. As Walsh was to recount later: "The weight shown not only wiped out the 'factor of safety' but exceeded the theoretical resistance of the foundation."

The commissioner couldn't believe his own figures at first. Surely the architect could not be guilty of such an error, Walsh reasoned. He burned his figures and forgot the matter for ten days. Then, still haunted by the specter of the dome falling one day

and obliterating the seat of government, he reexamined the plan.

Walsh carefully made new estimates. The figures were the same. This time he gave his findings to General Walker, the project superintendent, and Walker agreed that they were correct. When they presented the problem to Wilke, the contractor said the question of the dome's safety had been bothering him for months. Any action, however, would have to come from the Capitol Board.

Walsh outlined the problem at the next meeting of the Capitol Board. The election in the preceding November, however, had given that body new members from the governor down. Walsh had been succeeded by R. M. Hall, and only State Treasurer Francis Lubbock had served previously. The new board members had not yet taken their seats, and those retiring preferred to leave the problem to their successors.

When the new board failed to take any action on the dome after two meetings, Walsh went directly to the new governor, Lawrence Sullivan Ross. The governor asked Walsh to submit his concerns in writing and Lawrence released it to the press.

Ross took action immediately by calling in three expert architects for their opinions: B. M. Harrod of New Orleans, N. J. Clayton of Galveston, and Eugene T. Heiner of Houston. They were asked to make a thorough investigation of the dome and recommend remedial measures.

The three agreed that the brick lining was too heavy and suggested that it be replaced with an elaborate system of iron braces. This was done, and the dome was completed as it is today. In their final report, the architectural experts also took a look at the entire building and concluded with these words:

> . . . The building throughout complies with the plans, specifications and contracts, evincing the intelligent and conscientious care of those in charge of the work, and when completed, will serve as a worthy Capitol of a great state.

(lrhp)
Group photograph of most of the sixty-two Scots who worked on the Capitol. Scottish stonemasons were brought from Scotland especially for the building of the Capitol due to a labor strike and boycott by the International Association of Granite Cutters. Twenty-four of the original eighty-six workers decided against coming to Texas and complied with the Alien Contract Labor Law of February 1885 when they arrived in New York.

(above)
Scottish stone cutters at the shaping yard. These workers, paid four dollars per day, crafted one of the most beautiful public buildings in the world.

(above)

Workers take a break and pose in front of the steam-powered engine or "donkey engine" used to move the huge granite blocks when they arrived in Austin. Note the boiler, chimney, and railroad tracks at left. This engine was used to lift the very heaviest objects in the Capitol's construction. The large wheel, called a "bull wheel," was used in conjunction with the derrick booms.

(urhp)

Convicts at the quarry site channel off slabs of granite to be formed into the building blocks of the Capitol. The granite was all taken from this same area of the giant granite batholith to ensure as close a color match as possible.

(lrhp)

Convicts with mule-drawn rail cars haul granite that has been quarried. According to a report by Adam Johnson in 1932: "On one occasion, a convict capable of operating the little locomotive, and a few of his companions, seized some children of the captain of the guards, held them as shields, mounted the locomotive that was near at hand, and made for the outside world. They gave the guards a merry chase for a while, but I believe they were all captured. Possibly some of them were killed, but no harm came to the children concerned."

(above)
Photograph showing supervised placement of a finished column on the third story of the north side of the Capitol. This general area would eventually be the balcony area for the State Library.

(urhp)
Three floors of the Capitol are finished. The small gingerbread house in front is that of the contractor of the Capitol, Abner Taylor, although Gus Wilke had taken Abner Taylor's place as general contractor by the time the cornerstone was placed. Abner Taylor assumed duties as manager of the XIT Ranch.

(lrhp)
The fourth floor of the Capitol with its attic areas is started. In the right portion of the Capitol, the glass roof line of the Senate skylight is apparent. All ten of the gin poles for the construction are visible in this photograph, and stairs are in place. The major portion of the structural steel and ornamental ironwork for the Capitol was imported from Belgium.

(ulhp)
Photograph taken from the Governor's Mansion in August 1887, showing the start of the iron framework construction for the dome. Part of the roofing is completed and the central frame for the dome has been started. Most of the structural steel for the dome came from Belgium. Originally, cast iron was to be used on the exterior of the dome; however, on August 23, 1887, it was decided to substitute galvanized iron in that it would be much safer, lighter, and economical. Much of the brick lining of the dome was also deleted and metal was used instead. The exterior shell of the dome is painted so that it appears to be granite from a distance.

(llhp)
Progress on the Capitol dome is shown in this photo taken from a northeastern vantage point. Twenty-four circular royal blue flashed glass pieces adorned the round windows in the structure to the right of the dome under construction. The interior finishing work of wainscoting and ornate-carved doorways is well under way.

(this page)
The unfinished dome, made in Austin, prior to attachment of exterior sheet metal. The copper roof has been attached. Much of the iron used in the dome and in the rest of the building was cast at the State Penitentiary in Rusk, Texas. A lighter-weight steel was used for the shell, with pillars of cast iron and much of the decorative work done in zinc. Architects B. M. Harrod of New Orleans, N. J. Clayton of Galveston, and E. T. Heiner of Houston were employed to make sure the dome was safe and properly constructed. (Notice the man on the scaffold about halfway up the dome in this picture.)

View from the Capitol grounds looking south down Congress Avenue. The ornate building on the left is the old Travis County Courthouse and the building on the right is, of course, the temporary Capitol. The avenue is still unpaved, and city streetcars using the track in the middle of the street are still horse-drawn. Telegraph lines are strung along the left side of Congress Avenue.

12

The Ascension of a Goddess—Or a Pig?

The builders of such a "worthy Capitol" felt that the finishing touch should be a fitting ornament to perch on the dome 311 feet above the grounds. Their choice was the "Goddess of Liberty," a statue of a lady with a face that only a mother or a true Texan could love.

Even fans of the Goddess agree that she would almost surely place last in any beauty contest. However, her presence atop the dome is welcomed when one considers what might have been. In 1852, three decades before Texas became concerned about building a new capitol, it was seriously suggested that the headquarters of the state be adorned with the likeness of a pig!

The idea of a porker being given a place of honor above the seat of government did not originate with a Texan. It came from the same respected Philadelphia banker quoted in an earlier chapter as believing that the capital should have remained in Houston. William M. Gouge wasn't trying to be humorous when he proposed the unique statue in his book, *The Fiscal History of Texas . . . From the Commencement of the Revolution to 1834 to 1852, Etc.* In it, he argued: "As Rome was saved by the cackling of geese, so Texas was saved by the squealing of pigs."

He was referring to an incident in 1841, when the butchering of a hog by the servant of an angry French diplomat was a factor in France's refusal to lend the broke Republic of Texas $5 million.

France had a legation in Austin at the time— the only foreign government to have such formal representation in the new nation. The *charge d'affaires,* a suave diplomat named Alphonse Dubois de Saligny, also was a gardener of some ability. So when five pigs owned by Richard Bullock, who ran a Congress Avenue hotel, wandered onto the legation grounds and obliterated Saligny's fine vegetables, he ordered a servant to kill one of the intruders.

Bullock, who prized his porkers over any garden, retaliated by thrashing the servant. The matter became a diplomatic incident.

Unfortunately, it all happened while James Hamilton, a special envoy from Texas, was in Paris trying to negotiate a loan that the fledgling Republic needed desperately. The French, concerned that Texas might become overly friendly with both Britain and the U.S., seemed the likeliest source of such funds.

Diplomat Saligny, until the pig incident, also favored the loan from his government. However, his reasons were not altogether altruistic. He got his friends in the Texas Congress to introduce a bill which would, in exchange for the loan, grant France three million acres of land. In turn, France would bring in 8,000 immigrants, build a string of forts, be allowed to work all mines in Texas, and have the sole right of trade with Mexico.

There Were Lobbyists Then, Too

Saligny saw the deal as his chance to become the *empresario* who would bring in the settlers. He also believed that it would make France the dominant force in Texas and that both he and his government would prosper. An astute lobbyist, he used the legation to try and sell members of Congress on the idea.

Each night, he filled the legation with political leaders of the Republic. He hoped that his superb table, fine wines, and the best cigars would win votes for his proposal. Sam Houston and other prominent Texans already supported it.

But President Mirabeau B. Lamar and Vicepresident David G. Burnet opposed the idea. Along with many congressmen, they saw it as a massive land grab by France in exchange for a comparatively small loan. Texas needed the money, but not at the cost of what many believed would be the eventual loss of its freedom. The Fifth Congress defeated the bill.

Saligny wasn't defeated, however. He got the Sixth Congress to consider a new bill that also guaranteed his right to be *empresario*. It not only would assure him of potential riches but would pave the way for French control of Texas. The diplomat believed that "he who has the gold, rules" — and France had the gold.

Then came the incident with Bullock's pigs. Most Texans sided with the Austin innkeeper; so did the majority of the Sixth Congress. That body turned down Saligny's proposal. Angered at this action, Saligny closed the legation, left Austin, and the loan was never negotiated.

Five Pigs Cost $5 Million

Loss of the $5 million had no visible effect on the affairs of the Republic of Texas. Looking at the matter a decade later in Philadelphia, banker Gouge thought it was the best thing that could have happened. He also was certain that the loan, if consummated, would have given France eventual control of Texas.

Hence he was inspired to suggest that a statue of a pig be placed over the entrance to the treasury of Texas. Gouge wrote that "It would serve as memento to future ages of his [the pig] having been the salvation of Texas . . . and that the humblest of agents may be instrumental in producing consequences of the utmost importance."

Is She or Is She Not the "Mystery Lady"?

Gouge's suggestion was forgotten, or at least ignored, when the Capitol Board got around to selecting an adornment for the building's dome. Their choice was the figure of a woman who stands fifteen feet, seven and a half inches from the sole of her sandals to the star she holds aloft in her left hand. Designed by the architect, Elijah E. Myers, as part of his original Capitol plan, she has been known for more than a century as the "Goddess of Liberty."

That Myers was inspired by a similar image atop the national Capitol in Washington is a certainty. That one, called "Freedom" and sculpted by Thomas Crawford, was placed there in 1863. "Freedom" is the taller of the two (nineteen feet, six inches), and

unlike the Texas statue, has refined, classical facial features.

The Goddess of Liberty is no lady fair. Her face resembles that of a woman of eighty; in fact, the workmen who helped erect her originally referred to her affectionately as "The Old Lady." She is of muscular build, has a square, protruding jaw, stern and unyielding eyes, and thick hair that hangs low on her forehead. A plaited strand hangs over her left shoulder.

For a crown, she wears a wreath of olive branches. In addition to the star she holds over her head in her left hand, there is an unsheathed sword in her right hand pointing down. She is dressed in a flowing robe like those worn by the deities of ancient Greece, and hence has been called "goddess."

She has never been confused with the goddess of beauty. Two months after the statue was erected on February 26, 1888, some Austin women petitioned Governor Ross to furnish her "with a hat, a feather and a bustle. As she now is, she is a reproach to us."

There is one theory to explain her ugliness: the artist had to exaggerate her features so they would be visible to those who stood more than 300 feet away. Her overweight body was deliberate to reflect the Victorian tastes of the times.

Beautiful or not, the lady always has had an air of mystery surrounding her. There are two very different stories even as to how the Goddess of Liberty was created. One source indicates that the sculptor was an unknown Belgian. Some newspapers of the period trace her origin to France, Spain, and even Pennsylvania, while others never attempted to assign her nativity. These articles describe her variously as having been cast in bronze, white bronze, and zinc, and assign her heights ranging from fourteen to nineteen feet.

The name of her sculptor has never surfaced, but there is no doubt that the molds from which the Goddess was cast were made in Chicago by the firm of Friedley & Voshardt. A foundry had been established in the basement of the new Capitol, and the statue was cast there in zinc from the molds shipped to Austin by train. Later assembled on the grounds, the completed figure was then hoisted atop the dome.

One account says this was accomplished with one of the derricks used to move the blocks of granite and limestone. However, the *Austin American-Statesman* reported on February 18, 1888 — a week before the statue was put in place — that the last of these derricks had been taken down that day. Assuming that story to be accurate, it is likely that a section of the dome roof was left uncovered so that the Goddess could be lifted in four pieces to the top of the dome through the rotunda.

The Goddess would remain perched above the dome for ninety-seven years. Age took its toll. Efforts to protect her were made, of course. She was repainted her original white several times, repainted in blue at least once and her star in gold (although the colors didn't show up too well from the street), and later painted white again.

In the summer and fall of 1985, it became apparent that paint as a cosmetic was not enough. The Goddess had aged to a point where she had become a safety hazard. The State Preservation Board, concerned that the Goddess might be in need of plastic surgery or more, called in Washington University Technology Associates, Inc., of St. Louis to give her a complete physical examination. Once the experts had checked her aging anatomy, their verdict was ominous. There was no way to put her oversized zinc body into shape to last another century. The only answer was to clone her.

On October 23 it was announced that the days of the aging lady were numbered. On November 24 a helicopter removed her from the dome.

The High Cost of Beautifying a Goddess

The Goddess was carefully shipped to the American Art Foundry at Rhome. In this quiet community west of Fort Worth in Wise County, her tired body was taken apart and cleaned thoroughly. New molds were made and sent to Dellray Bronze, Inc., of Houston, where experts recast the Goddess in aluminum just as she had appeared originally. The cost was more than $450,000, all from private sources. Gifts poured in from all over Texas, including donations from hundreds of school students.

When the reincarnation was complete, the new Goddess made her debut with a brief tour. Her first stop was San Antonio and the Alamo where, for eight hours, she was displayed to the delight of hundreds of citizens and tourists. Then she went to Rockdale, the aluminum capital of the state, so workers there could see what that metal had wrought. A Texas National Guard helicopter crew then flew her to Austin to place her back on her pedestal atop the Capitol.

In the pre-helicopter days a century ago, workmen building the Capitol apparently had few problems in getting the Goddess to her pinnacle on the dome. But this was not the case in 1986.

The first attempts to place the new Goddess of Liberty were made on May 31. Tricky winds, low clouds, and the inability of the pilots to see the statue as it swung from the aircraft made the efforts a failure. Newspapers reported that at least sixteen attempts were made the first day before the pilots gave up.

On June 1 there was a second try. Repeated efforts were made by the CH-47 "Chinook" crew to gently lower the swaying, 2,900-pound statue onto a seven-inch-wide vertical rod that was to be its base atop the dome. Again winds and weather (the cloud ceiling dropped from 1,800 to 400 feet) defeated the attempts.

The crew had overlooked the vagaries of Texas weather. It was reported that the pilots had practiced for two months using an object about the same size and weight of the statue "and had never missed it." The unpredictable winds around the dome of the 311-foot-tall building proved their undoing when they tried the real thing. Visibility was even a more serious problem. Despite the aid of a TV monitor mounted in the cockpit, the pilots had difficulty seeing the statue dangling in its nylon harness thirty-five feet below the aircraft. As Governor Mark White told the press, "It has been aptly described as trying to thread a needle without being able to see the thread or the needle."

Also, the CH-47 was not the ideal helicopter for the job. Fortunately, Mississippi—one of the states that had helped Sam Houston win Texas its independence in 1836—had exactly the craft which was needed. As any good neighbor should, that state offered its help.

On June 14, with better weather and the Mississippi National Guard CH-54 "Skycrane" doing the transporting, Goddess of Liberty II was placed on her pedestal on the first pass of the aircraft. A crowd of more than 5,000 which had gathered on the Capitol grounds cheered as the "Old Lady" was settled into her accustomed place, ready to watch over the seat of Texas government for another century or more.

And what of the original Goddess of Liberty? Not only has she been replaced by a younger woman, but she has had her faced turned to the wall in lonely storage within a state-owned hangar at an Austin airport.

The State Preservation Board originally planned to keep her around. She was scheduled to go on display in the Capitol rotunda. Then, early in 1988, it was decided to put her in storage, at least until restoration plans for the Capitol are completed sometime in the future. For the centennial celebration she was temporarily placed on display outside the south entrance on the east side of the Capitol building.

Perhaps one day the "Old Lady" will have a place of honor inside the building she watched over for so many years or have a new home befitting her stature.

The 1888 Capitol is basically complete, though the Goddess of Liberty has not been placed atop her perch. Texas has the unique distinction of having the only state capitol which was not paid for directly with the taxpayers' money.

(above)
Workers, supervisors, and dignitaries (including City Marshal Ben Thompson to the immediate right of the statue) gather for a group photograph with the Goddess of Liberty on February 23, 1888. Many names have been attributed to the statue including the Goddess of Liberty, the Statue of Liberty, the Goddess of Victory, the Goddess of Wisdom, the Lady, and Old Lady. The fifteen-foot-tall statue was cast in three sections of zinc. Her mysteries are numerous, and she silently overlooks her monument to all Texans.

(left)
Excerpt from 1897 Friedley and Voshardt catalogue of architectural sheet metal ornaments and statues that was printed in Chicago, Illinois. Identified as Statue No. 453, this mold was the basis for the Goddess of Liberty that was cast in zinc and placed atop the Texas State Capitol.

81

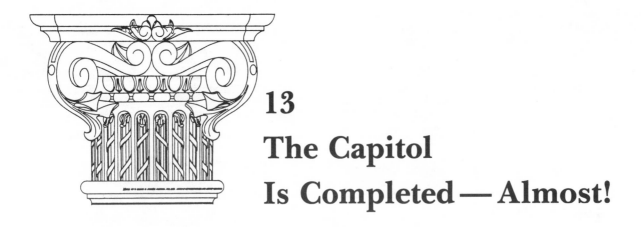

13

The Capitol
Is Completed — Almost!

On February 26, 1888, when the original Goddess was hoisted atop the dome, the new Capitol was virtually complete. At least, the contractors hoped and believed that it was.

Six years had elapsed since the ground was broken for the building, and work had progressed rapidly as the project neared its end. In January 1888, some 85,000 square feet of copper had been put in place to complete the roof, covering a building that is 585 feet, 10 inches in length and 299 feet, 10 inches wide. The interior woods are oak, pine, cherry, cedar, walnut, ash, and mahogany. The original floors were of hand-blocked clay tile, glass, and wood, but many of these were replaced in 1936 with terrazzo.

When completed, the Capitol was said to be the seventh largest building under a single roof in the world. More than 1,000 workers had labored, often day and night, to finish the job. And on April 16, the commissioners formally notified Governor Ross and the Capitol Board that the "solid, substantial, magnificent and imposing State House was now ready for a thorough inspection." It would soon appear that such a check was sorely needed.

However, the 20th Legislature, meeting in special session, passed an act authorizing the board to accept or reject, "in whole or in part," the new building. The members also were authorized to proceed with plans for its dedication.

The board acted quickly. On May 8, members voted to accept the Capitol with these exceptions: inside blinds, iron stairways on the east and west ends of the building, and a drainage system remained to be installed. The contractor agreed promptly to correct these deficiencies, and May 16 was selected as the date for the formal dedication.

However, more problems were still to come, and months would pass before Texas would finally be pleased with its new Capitol.

Dedicatory Ceremonies Were Dampened

On the day of the dedication of the Capitol, Austin had a population of about 14,000. At least 20,000 were on hand for the ceremonies, however, as proud citizens poured in from around the state. Texans had waited thirty-nine years since the selection of the capital site for the completion of a permanent building to house their government, and they were ready to celebrate.

They didn't wait until the May 16 formal dedication to come to Austin. Hundreds took advantage of the cent-a-mile excursion rate offered by the railroads and came early. As a result, the festivities actually started May 14 and extended through May 19.

Accommodations were sparse, but every effort was made to extend hospitality to the largest crowd Austin had entertained up to that time. A tent city had been erected on a flat plain more than a mile west of the Capitol. The encampment abutted the International & Great Northern Railway tracks, and a streetcar line had been hastily laid to help move the crowds to and from Congress Avenue.

Entertainment was almost constant from dawn to late evening for the five days. There were baseball games, an exhibition of wild cattle roping, band concerts by the dozen, and presentations by German choral groups. Special days had been set aside to honor special groups, such as the Farmers Alliance, ranchers, cowboys, and others.

As might be expected in such an atmosphere of carnival, there were dozens of hawkers offering everything from beer and ice cream to souvenirs. Sheet music copies of the "State Capitol Waltz," with an elegant picture of the new Capitol on the cover, sold for sixty cents. Specimens of dressed granite from the quarry that produced the Capitol stone were available as permanent mementoes of the occasion. For those who wanted to see the quarry close up, the railroad offered round-trip excursions to Burnet County for $2.

Competitive military drills were performed by groups like the Louisville Light Infantry from Kentucky and the Robert E. Lee Rifles from Montgomery, Alabama. Fireworks displays were presented by world-famous pyrotechnists from London.

It was a field day for the press. The *Austin American-Statesman* printed more than 10,000 copies of the paper on May 16 and sold all of them before the dedicatory program ended. The *Houston Post,* not to be outdone, published a special twenty-four page edition, which it handed out free to visitors, along with a beautiful cape jasmine bud for the ladies.

At the formal ceremonies on May 16, Governor Ross presided. He introduced a host of dignitaries, including Senator A. W. Terrell, author of the bill authorizing Texas to trade public lands for the construction of its Capitol. Terrell gave the welcoming address, followed by Col. Abner Taylor. As the representative of the contracting Capitol Syndicate, Taylor formally presented the building to the people of Texas.

The dedicatory address was delivered by Temple Houston, youngest son of the hero of San Jacinto. Houston, a lawyer, orator, plainsman, and legislator, had another unique distinction: he was the first child to be born in the Texas Governor's Mansion.

Among all of the orations in the annals of Texas, the one delivered by old Sam's son in dedicating the Capitol rates as one of the most colorful. Houston used the occasion to give his listeners a lesson in Texas history because, he told the audience, "reason ordains a brief reference to the deeds and times that eventuate this occasion."

He congratulated the Capitol Syndicate, not only for "this magnificent building that will speak for their skill for thousands of years," but also for turning "previously useless land" into a state monument. He paid tribute to the building itself with these stirring words:

The architecture of a civilization is its most enduring feature, and by this structure shall Texas

transmit herself to posterity, for here science has done her utmost. The quarry has given up its granite, and the mines have yielded their brass and iron, and an empire has been passed as an equivalent of this house . . . It would seem that here glitters a structure that shall stand as a sentinel of eternity, to gaze upon passing ages, and surviving, shall mourn as each star expires . . .

Houston finished his speech to thunderous applause. When Governor Ross arose for his, a sudden rainstorm roared over Austin and a heavy shower drenched the place. To the consternation of everyone, the building which Houston had predicted "shall stand as a sentinel of eternity" was capped by a roof that leaked like a sieve.

The New Capitol is Rejected

The crowds which had gathered with such pride to dedicate their new Capitol were furious. The building which Temple Houston had called a "noble edifice" to bequeath to future generations was unable to withstand a Texas rainstorm. It was a problem that demanded an immediate solution, but it became mired in red tape. In fact, it was four months before the matter was even given official consideration.

In late August, Gen. W. P. Hardeman, who had been named superintendent of buildings and grounds, completed a personal study of the Capitol. As early as June, he had complained that the basement windows would not close properly. Now he spent weeks compiling a critical report in which he blamed the commissioners and the contractor for a long list of deficiencies.

Hardeman admitted that he was not familiar with the plans and specifications. However, he knew exactly what he expected the building to be when completed, and he picked on every error in design and construction that he could find.

As expected, the commissioners replied with a five-page answer of their own in which they defended their own actions. They also took a verbal swipe at the superintendent when they said:

We . . . do not regard Mr. Hardeman as being capable of understanding the maps, as he calls them, of this building. We are sustained in this opinion by Mr. Hardeman's own confession . . . We have always urged and still insist that if our work is to be criticized it shall be done by those capable of doing so.

Hardeman found a partial ally in R. L. Walker, who had supervised the construction. On August 28, Walker charged that the Capitol Board had not accepted expert advice. He agreed that the material, workmanship, and finish of the leaking roof had been carried out exactly in accordance with a supplemental contract made by order of the board a year before the building's completion. In that contract, over the protests of Walker and Gus Wilke, the contractor's supervisor, the board specified that copper be used instead of slate for the roof.

Both Walker and Wilke had pointed out that copper expands and contracts with weather changes and predicted that this would cause leaks. The board used the copper against their advice.

Wilke to the Rescue Again

Although Wilke could not see why he was being held responsible for the roof when he had protested the use of copper, he wrote the board on September 4 and offered to replace it at his own expense. In his letter, he said,

> The proposition is made for two reasons. The one is that with a bad roof on this structure, no matter how it got there, it will not be a credit to have built this magnificent building, spending six of the best years of my life in the undertaking. I cannot afford to have anything seriously wrong with any part of this building, whether I was to blame or not. And the other reason is, that if my proposition is accepted, it will enable me to have a settlement of my contract with the Chief Contractor.

Two days later, the Reception Board (which was the old Capitol Board minus the attorney general) met and refused to accept Wilke's offer. He then offered "to keep the copper roof in good repair for a term of three years" and the board rejected that offer. They also continued to refuse to accept the building.

Attorney General James Stephen Hogg also en-tered the argument. He not only opposed accepting the building but urged board members who disagreed with that position to resign. Instead of resigning, the board, with the blessing of the Capitol Syndicate, employed Edward C. Miller, a nationally known architect of Washington, D.C., to inspect the building. He was told to determine whether or not "it was first class in every respect." Both the Capitol Board and the contractor agreed to accept his findings.

Miller reported several minor discrepancies and these were easily remedied. He also decided that the defects in the roof "were not of so serious a character as rumor suggested." He pointed these out to Wilke and directed him to make repairs with solder. The architect warned that the roof would always require periodic inspection, but that maintenance would pose no problems. It hasn't, but the roof does leak occasionally.

On December 7, 1888, Miller met with the board and recommended that the building be finally accepted. The next day, almost seven years after the first ground was broken, Texas had its new Capitol at last. The Capitol Syndicate was released from its contract and given clear title to the remainder of the three million acres due the partners.

In return for the land, Texas gained a Capitol which cost $3,774,630.60. The state assumed more than half a million of that expense, and the Capitol Syndicate picked up the remaining $3,224,593.45. Thus the state doubled its money, receiving a value of more than a dollar an acre for land that it valued at only half that at the time. The trade appeared to be an even better bargain than the state had hoped to get in the beginning.

In one sense, it still is a bargain. Only when those three million acres are valued in 1988 dollars does the magnificent statehouse seem an extravagance. Not only is the land which Texas valued at $1.5 million in 1882 worth billions today, but it produces far more in income each year than its estimated worth more than a century ago.

(rhp)
The front cover of *The Chicago Illustrated Graphic News* dated Tuesday, November 1, 1887, tells of the proposed grand military and civic celebration to be held in Austin during May of 1888. Preparations were obviously well under way more than six months before the dedication. The Dedication Committee reported that newspapers both in Texas and outside the state had been very kind.

THE · CHICAGO · ILLUSTRATED ·

GRAPHIC · NEWS

VOL. VIII, No. 15.   CHICAGO, TUESDAY, NOVEMBER 1, 1887.   TERMS: {Ten Cents per Copy. {$2.50 per Year, in Advance.

AUSTIN, TEXAS—THE PROPOSED GRAND MILITARY AND CIVIC CELEBRATION TO BE GIVEN IN HONOR OF THE COMPLETION
AND DEDICATION OF THE TEXAS STATE HOUSE, IN MAY, 1888. (See Page 229.)

Harper's Weekly article of May 12, 1888, foretelling completion of the new Capitol of Texas. Portraits of Sam Houston and Stephen F. Austin bear prominent positions above a perspective of the statehouse. It is understated in the article that "The new Texas Capitol, of which Austin is the seat, is one of the finest red granite buildings in the world."

(this page)
1911 Capitol view from Congress Avenue. This is one of a planned series of five paintings covering the Capitol and the downtown area in 1888, 1911, 1936, 1961, and 1986. The originals are oils measuring two by three feet. *(Painting by Bob Langkop)*

About the Cover
G. Harvey brings Texas history to life in his oil painting, "Streetcars Along the Avenue." This magnificent rendition of the Capitol shows the early 1900s when the age of electricity, streetcars, and city automation challenged and changed the traditional way of life for the cowboy and turn-of-the-century Texans.

(above)
1936 Lone Star Capitol depicting Congress Avenue
and the Statehouse during the Texas Centennial. Each painting in the series is intended to show the spirit and the times
during the Capitol's first hundred years.

(Painting by Bob Langkop)

(right)
"Parade 150" watercolor was inspired by the Sesquicenten-
nial Parade up Congress Avenue towards the Capitol. The
horseman symbolizes the Lone Texas Ranger of our Lone
Star State. The mixture of old and new buildings catches
the flavor of present-day Austin.

(Watercolor by Mary Doerr)

The "Dawn at the Alamo" painting by H. A. McArdle
(1836–1908). Thirty years of research and five years of painting went into the creation of this incredibly accurate historical painting. The Battle of the Alamo was the famous en-
counter of 183 Texans commanded by Col. William B. Travis
with an army of over 2,400 Mexicans commanded by General Santa Anna. The siege lasted thirteen days. Finally, at
dawn on March 6, 1836, the Mexican army took the Alamo.
All of the Texans, as well as 1,000 of Santa Anna's men, lost
their lives. It was a pyric victory for the Mexican army as
told in William B. Travis' last letter from the Alamo to the
President of the Convention dated March 1, 1836:

> I will do the best I can under the circumstances;
> if we lose, the victory will cost the enemy so dear,
> that it will be worse to him than a defeat . . . God
> and Texas — Victory or Death.

"The Battle of San Jacinto" painting by H. A. McArdle. This historical painting hangs in the Texas Senate Chamber along with the "Dawn at the Alamo" painting by the same artist. It depicts the surprise attack by Gen. Sam Houston and his army during the Mexican army's siesta hour, April 21, 1836. Two of Houston's men were killed at the battle, Pvt. Lemuel Stockton and 2nd Lt. George Lamb, and seven more died later of wounds. Twenty-three were wounded. Santa Anna lost 630 men and 730 men were taken prisoner. The artist spent years of research on this painting and took seven years to paint the historic portrayal.

The "Surrender of Santa Anna" by William Henry Huddle (1847–1892). This painting recreates Gen. Antonio López de Santa Anna's capture and surrender to Gen. Sam Houston on April 22, 1836, the day following the Battle of San Jacinto. Sam Houston lies on a blanket with a wounded leg and Deaf Smith is shown cupping his ear while Santa Anna, in white pants at Houston's feet, accepts an armistice.

THE NEW CAPITOL OF TEXAS

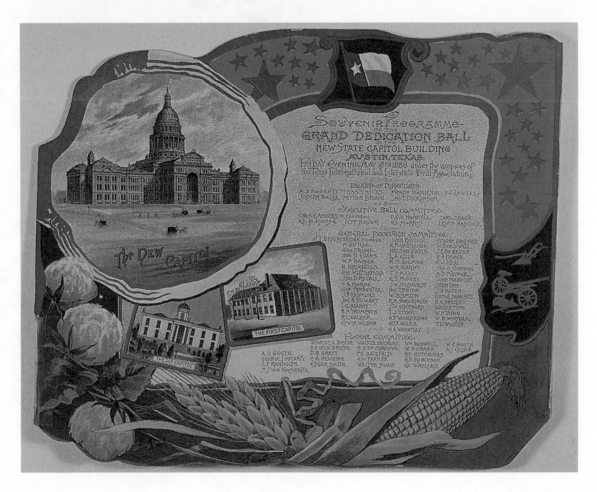

The New Capitol

The Old Capitol

THE FIRST CAPITOL

Souvenir Programme
GRAND DEDICATION BALL
NEW STATE CAPITOL BUILDING
AUSTIN, TEXAS.
FRIDAY EVENING MAY 16TH 1888 under the auspices of
the Texas International and Interstate Drill Association.

(preceding page top)
The dedication of the Texas State Capitol. Color newspaper reproduction of the State Capitol taken from E. E. Myers's perspective of the building. The pictures surrounding the Capitol are of Texas heroes from the Republic era, of the Alamo, and of the Old Capitol at Houston. It is interesting that the description starts out "The building is to be a fire-proof structure . . ." The dedication proved to be a gala affair that took place on May 16, 1888; however, it was actually a week long affair of activities starting May 14 and continuing through May 19.

(preceding page bottom)
Detailed color souvenir program for the grand dedication ball in 1888. At the actual dedication of the Capitol, Senator Temple Houston made these comments about the history of instability of our state government seat: "Texas has changed the site of her government more than any other state in the union, or any nation on this side of the globe. Prior to the transfer of this building the site of government of Texas has been changed eleven times."

(this page)
Watercolor perspective of the Texas State Capitol, drawn by E. E. Myers. Several features seen on this perspective were omitted during the Capitol construction due to cost and changes in materials. The most notable change was made in substituting granite for the poor grade of limestone. Other changes included the elimination of the east and west porticoes, the roof being covered with copper instead of slate, elimination of some of the more ornate stone carvings, omission of many of the decorative finials, and constructing the wainscoting of wood instead of marble.

Statue of Stephen Fuller Austin in the entrance foyer of the Texas Capitol. This Italian marble statue of Austin was sculpted by German-born Elisabet Ney in 1901. Stephen F. Austin, referred to as "the Father of Texas" was born in Virginia. He helped to establish the first English-speaking colony in Texas and was the first secretary of state of the Republic of Texas.

Marble statue of Sam Houston in the entrance foyer of the Capitol. The statue was sculpted by Elisabet Ney (1833–1907), a brilliant sculptress who left Germany in 1870 for the United States and in 1892 built a studio in Austin.

LIBERTY OR DEATH.

(this page)
The beautiful and original Battle Flag of San Jacinto displayed in the Texas House of Representatives chamber. Known as Miss Liberty, the woman on this flag was originally almost completely nude. However, when the flag was given to the State of Texas, it was mended, treated, "clothed," and framed to hang in the House chamber. In one hand Miss Liberty carries a sword draped with a banner inscribed "Liberty or Death." *(Photo by Bill Malone)*

(next two pages)
Northeastern view of sunset over the Capitol capturing the "violet crown" effect that blesses the Austin skies. This beautiful photograph of the Capitol exemplifies one of the many moods of magnificence that the building assumes. *(Photo by Barbara Schlief © copyright)*

Fall settles in around the Capitol. This autumn shot was taken
from the southeast.

Splendid night photograph of the Capitol when the lighted
star still shone on the south pediment of the building.

Parade on Congress Avenue preceding the dedication of the Capitol on May 16, 1888. The *Austin Daily Statesman* estimated that approximately 20,000 people were on hand for the dedication ceremonies. The 10,000 special copies of the newspaper, printed for the event, were sold out by 11:00 A.M. Austin was packed for the auspicious occasion. The *Daily Statesman* of May 17 reported: "The great and magnificent State Capitol building was yesterday dedicated with a splendor that was befitting the glory of Texas and the grandeur of that building . . . It was a memorable, a glorious day. A day to be inscribed in the history of a great commonwealth."

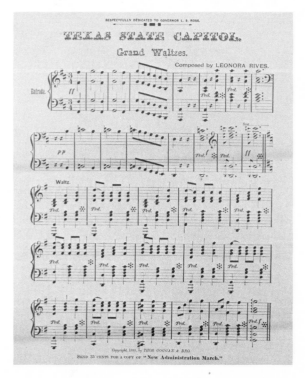

(above)
One of the most popular souvenirs available from the dedication was the "Texas State Capitol Grand Waltz," which sold for sixty cents a copy. This sheet music was composed by Leonora Rives, especially for the dedication of the Capitol. The song was published by Thomas Goggan and Brothers of Galveston and dedicated to the first governor to occupy the Capitol, Lawrence Sullivan Ross.

(left)
First page of the "Texas State Capitol Grand Waltz." This Victorian piece of music was played at the grand dedication ball. Austin went all out to celebrate this crowning achievement in Texas history.

Elaborate dance program from the grand dedication ball used by the ladies to keep record of their dance partners. Note the small pencil attached for that purpose.

Aerial view of Austin in 1888. On April 21, 1888, the fifty-second anniversary of the Battle of San Jacinto, the Capitol building was first opened to the public. In 1890 the city of Austin had an official census population of 14,575 and proudly possessed the seventh largest building in the world, its new statehouse.

14

The Finishing Touches

A building with an opulent interior like the Capitol's deserved to be furnished with matching elegance. Such was certainly the intent of the legislature. Late in 1887, as the building neared completion, a Capitol Furnishing Board was established and $100,000 appropriated for its use.

In a time when a good cigar cost a nickel, restaurants served coffee free with twenty-five-cent meals, and butchers cheerfully gave away the liver from their shops, $100,000 seemed a generous allotment. However, there are almost 200,000 square feet of public space in the Capitol, and the Furnishing Board (which also was charged with landscaping the grounds) soon discovered that it had a budget problem.

Today's State Purchasing and General Services Commission would be ecstatic if it could buy at prices anywhere near the level of the bids that came in to furnish the Capitol in 1888. For example, the Fenton Metallic and Manufacturing Co. of Chicago agreed to provide "roller shelving, file cases and letter cabinets" for every office in the building for only $25,000.

For another $20,000, the A. H. Andrews Co. of the same city provided rugs and mats for the rooms and draperies and shades for the 924 windows. The same firm agreed to provide desks and other needed furniture for all offices for $52,000.

Although these prices seem to be unbelievable bargains a century later, they were devastating to the plans of the Furnishing Board. Even with the help of an expert buyer, N. J. Clayton of Galveston, the board could not stretch its budget. When the members had spent their entire $100,000 appropriation, there were still forty-six bare rooms in the Capitol. Many months would pass before they were finally furnished and put into use.

Landscaping

While the Furnishing Board was trying to solve its problems with the building's interior, the legislature turned its attention to the grounds. Since the lawmakers seemed to feel that each aspect of the Capitol's completion needed its own set of overseers, they created a Board for Fencing and Improving the Grounds. Governor Sul Ross decided to chair it himself and named Attorney General Hogg and Building Superintendent Hardeman to serve with him.

With its usual generosity, the legislature appropriated $35,000 to fence and landscape the almost twenty-six acres of lawn around the building. This figure also was meant to include the building of walks and drives. The highlight was to be an ornamental wrought-iron metal fence laced with 8,282 gold-plated stars in bas relief.

The base of the fence was a small granite-on-limestone ledge around the perimeter of the grounds. Building the base took $22,786.62 of the appropriation. By the time Mast, Frost & Co. of Springfield, Ohio, had built and installed the enclosure, the board had spent $42,994.51. Records indicate that "other sources" provided the $8,000 that was spent in excess of the available funds. Most of the landscaping was simply postponed.

Lighting

The state's business wasn't conducted only during the day, so lighting the building and grounds loomed as another problem. The legislature appropriated another $11,360 for wiring and light fixtures. As in the cases of the furnishing and landscaping, however, the job couldn't be accomplished with the funds available.

Gas pipes to feed 3,200 lights already had been installed during the construction. However, a new power source called electricity had come along, and the lawmakers wanted their new Capitol to be as modern as possible. Existing lights were never connected to a gas line. Instead the state purchased an inadequate dynamo which could power only 650 lights — about a fifth of the outlets.

This was not a problem except when the legislature was in session. While both the House and Senate are often accused today of "being in the dark" on specific legislative matters, members in 1888 found little joy in working in the half light available. By 1892, they had seen to it that there was enough electricity to power 1,500 lights. It would be two more decades before the Capitol finally was connected to the city of Austin's generating plant. Then, for the first time in its history, Texas government had adequate light for its labors.

In an effort to save money, permanent lighting fixtures had been installed only in the chambers of the House of Representatives and Senate and the offices of the governor. In the legislative halls, chandeliers in the shape of the Texas star were designed and installed by H. C. Cooke of New York at a cost of $1,700. All other fixtures in the Capitol were of the "cheapest, temporary character" and remained so for many years.

Water was another unanticipated expense. The shrubbery, grass, and trees all had to have it to subsist, and the dyanamo required water for its operation. For another $9,902.61, the state was able to get a well drilled on the grounds. In time, the Capitol was hooked up to the mains of the city of Austin, the source of its water supply today.

Art

Despite the budget crunch, the legislature believed that the Capitol should be enhanced by art. Again these bodies created a Board to Purchase Pictures and gave them $10,000 to do so.

The board's first item of business was to order portraits of the former presidents of the Republic of Texas and of each governor since statehood. Among the first purchases were life-size portraits of Sam Houston and Thomas J. Rusk, painted by William Henry Huddle, one of the most prominent artists of the time.

In the intervening years, the Capitol has become a virtual art gallery. Dozens of paintings, sculptures, and other works have been added to the Capitol. Today the House and Senate chambers, the rotunda, and even the halls have become something of a museum. One painting which draws visitors from everywhere is Huddle's "Surrender of Santa Anna," which hangs in the south foyer.

Huddle's painting depicts Sam Houston, the wounded commander, arranging an armistice with Gen. Antonio López de Santa Anna, the vanquished dictator of Mexico, on April 22, 1836, the day after the Battle of San Jacinto assured independence from Mexico. The painting shows Santa Anna, after his capture in the uniform of a common soldier, being brought before Houston as he sat under a tree nursing his wounded leg.

The Grounds Become a Park

Just as new art objects are continually being acquired for the Capitol, landscaping and improving the spacious grounds is also an ongoing project. Today the grounds are shaded with more than 500 trees, including more than 50 varieties that are native to Texas. Included are pecan, sycamore, cottonwood, mesquite, mountain laurel, oak, hackberry, elm, walnut, peach, and cedar.

Two trees that became special attractions for visitors were known as the Jim Hogg pecans. They were planted on either side of the steps leading to the south, or main entrance, and were grown from nuts taken from the original memorial trees that mark the grave of the former governor in Austin's Oakwood Cemetery.

Hogg was especially fond of the pecan, the official tree of Texas. On his death, he directed that a pecan be planted at the head of his grave and another at the foot. His will directed that the product of these trees be distributed each year to "the common people of Texas." For many years after his death, pecans from the trees were sent to various county seats. Hundreds of "Jim Hogg pecans" still grace many courthouse squares and public school grounds.

Another unusual pecan tree stands near the north entrance. It grows in soil gathered from each of the state's 254 counties and is a memorial to Texan soldiers, sailors, and marines killed in World War II.

Also gracing the grounds are some of the finest sculptures in the state. During a century of development, many monuments for figures in history and for various causes have been placed on the acres of green lawns. One of the largest honors Jefferson Davis, president of the Confederate States of America, and memorializes the role of Texas in the Civil War. Another honors the Alamo heroes.

One of the most popular is a bronze depicting a Texas cowboy astride a bucking horse. There is also a greatly reduced replica of the Statue of Liberty; a bronze soldier representing Texas's part in the Spanish-American War; and a granite fountain commemorating the bicentennial of the United States. A granite tablet presented to the people of Texas in 1961 by the Fraternal Order of Eagles has the Ten Commandments etched on its face.

Although every effort is made to have everything about the Capitol and its grounds historically accurate, there is an occasional lapse. For example, twin cannons supposedly used in both the Texas Revolution and the Civil War guard the main entrance. A plaque says they were "Presented to the Republic of Texas by Major General T. J. Chambers — 1836."

This is not quite true. General Chambers, the same gentleman who claimed ownership of the land on which the Capitol stands and whose daughters finally settled their claim against the state in 1925, was not the donor of these guns. Neither were they used in the Texas Revolution; that war ended before the cannons ever reached Texas. They were, however, used in the Civil War.

It is true that the cannons were among six ordered by General Chambers during the revolt against Mexico. However, he did not purchase them. They were paid for with public funds. In 1836, Chambers asked McClung, Wade and Co., a Pittsburgh, Pennsylvania, foundry, to cast the guns. He was to pick them up in Cincinnati, Ohio, where they were to arrive by ship.

The foundry was slow in filling the order, however, and the cannons didn't get to the Ohio port until April 1837. By then the revolution had ended and Texas had been an independent Republic for a year. Nevertheless, Chambers accepted the guns and brought them to Galveston via New Orleans. Historical records do not indicate that the guns saw any action until the Civil War began in 1861.

High above the two cannons at the main entrance on the south and also above the north fascia are the only examples of what might be termed "art deco." In 1976, as a part of the Texas celebration of America's 200th birthday, the legislature decided to do something special. It ordered that colored mosaic seals of the six nations that had governed Texas be placed over the two entrances. The seals, executed and installed by Stasswender Marble and Granite Works of Austin, add colorful accents to the building.

During its second century, the Capitol and its grounds will continue to acquire works of art. By law, a portrait of each governor is added to the walls of the rotunda at the end of his or her term. Both the House and Senate chambers, already enhanced by dozens of historical paintings and mementoes like the San Jacinto Battle flag, will certainly add other items.

The spacious grounds, despite the many such items already there, have dozens of nooks and crannies left to support sculptures, monuments, and trees memorializing events from the future. Texans have never had any quarrel with their Capitol doubling as a museum and seem to relish each new acquisition. The mementoes and memorials already in place, and those that are sure to come, serve only to reinforce in the minds of Texas citizens the rich and colorful heritage that is theirs.

The Capitol Story
Part III

95

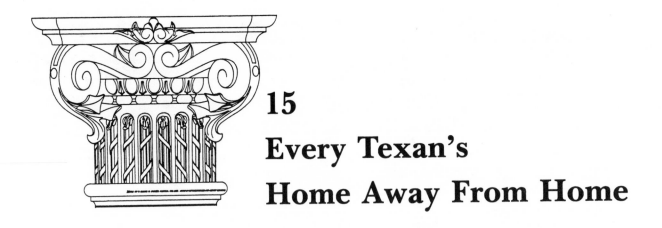

15

Every Texan's Home Away From Home

More than a million people a year visit the Capitol. One of the reasons they come is that the building is a living museum of Texas history as well as the nerve center of state government.

The House and Senate chambers and the Governor's reception room and office, all on the second floor, are magnets for visitors even when the legislature is not in session. Although the government itself has expanded into an adjoining complex of twelve high-rise buildings and more are on the way, it is the Capitol that remains the focus of attention.

Visitors never seem to tire of the building's outer and inner beauty. They admire its Doric architecture and the beautiful pink granite exterior. They marvel at its size. Built in the form of a Greek cross, it stretches the length of two football fields from east to west and almost half that from north to south. Once they enter by one of the wide doorways on each of the four sides and reach the point where the corridors cross, first-time visitors stop momentarily in the rotunda and stare in awe at the dome.

The large, circular chamber rises some 300 feet to the apex of the dome from which a gold lone star looks down onto the terrazzo floor below. That floor, installed in 1935, is said to be one of the largest in the world made by embedding pieces of granite and marble in mortar and then polishing it to a high gloss.

Floors: A History Walk

Floors in the Capitol have always been attractive. The first were of hand-blocked clay tile, glass, and wood. Most of the main floors installed in 1888 were richly colored encaustic tile supplied by an Indiana manufacturer. These refused to stay in place, however, and their constant lifting caused continu-

ing problems. Within a decade after the building's completion, most of the original tiles had been removed.

Originally, the rotunda floor beneath the dome was made of glass tiles in the shape of a hexagon. They were secured in a cast-iron frame and caulked with lead to make the surface watertight. Each tile was twelve inches square and an inch and a half thick. Surrounding the glass were bands of black, terra-cotta, and mauve-gray encaustic tiles which radiated from the center. The circular border around the rotunda was an ochre panel with a terra-cotta band.

The State Library quarters (moved years ago to its own beautiful building nearby) had a cast-iron and glass floor measuring fourteen by thirty feet. The second-floor facility also had a ceiling of embossed plate glass. There were well holes on the third and fourth floors, topped by a skylight and twenty-four circular windows glazed with royal blue flashed glass.

These so-called "well holes" had an artistic purpose. They admitted the soft, blue-tinted light all the way through the glass floor of the library and onto the northern corridor of the first floor. The holes remained in use until a renovation of the Capitol in the early 1970s.

The glass tiles were beautiful, but as traffic through the Capitol increased, engineers decided that they were a safety hazard. In 1922 a painter working on the fifth-floor balcony fell and crashed through the first-floor tiles and into the basement. It was not until 1935 that the legislature decided to replace the floors as one of the ways to celebrate the centennial of Texas's independence from Mexico.

C. H. Page of Austin was the architect for the project. Harold E. (Bubi) Jessen, another architect, did the design; a Denver contractor, the J. B. Martina

Mosaic Co., did the installation. Strip designs came from the Pascal Sylvester Co. of Chicago.

Perhaps the highlight of the entire first floor is the centerpiece of the rotunda. Created by the Art Mosaic and Tile Co. of Toledo, Ohio, it is a five-pointed Lone Star of Texas with the seal of the Republic of Texas (1836–1845) in the center. Seals of the other five nations whose flags have flown over Texas surround the star: Spain (1519–1821), France (1685–1762), Mexico (1821–1836), the Confederate States of America (1861–1865), and the United States (1845–1861 and 1865 to the present).

There are sixteen major colors of terrazzo flooring in the building, and all are used in the rotunda pattern. These include gold, silver, white, and black, plus varying shades of red, blue, yellow, green, and brown.

Building a new floor for the Capitol entirely of Texas stone was not easy. The design, for example, had to harmonize with the classicism of the building and still be perpetually modern. At the same time, it had to incorporate important aspects of the state's history in a tasteful manner.

Many Imperfections

There were physical problems also. Because the Capitol was built at a time when all construction was done by hand, measurements and spacing were anything but perfect. For example, there is as much as a six-inch variation in the placing of the columns in the corridors. At no two points are the widths of the halls exactly the same. Indeed, nothing is quite even or uniform anywhere in the building.

The floor motif has cleverly concealed many of these imperfections, an impressive accomplishment considering the problems with which the designers had to deal. Their success is evidenced by the fact that the terrazzo floors still draw plaudits from visiting artists and architects.

A major design problem resulted from the attempt to memorialize the twelve great battles in Texas history. Getting this done in an attractive, cohesive way was a challenge.

The battles depicted in the floor design represent three times of crisis in Texas history: the fight for independence from Mexico in the 1830s, the U.S. war with Mexico in the 1840s, and the American Civil War. On the floor of the south entrance, these battles have been divided into three groups. Over the

name of each are two crossed torches indicating that Texas was victorious.

In the center, the battles of the Alamo, Goliad, Gonzales, and San Jacinto commemorate Texas's struggle for independence.

The next group of battles memorialized are those of Bexar, Coleto, Palo Alto, and Sabine Pass. These are along the left wall of the corridor.

Other battles commemorated in the mosaics are worked into the terrazzo along the right side of the south foyer corridor. They include those of Anahuac, Velasco, Palmito, and Galveston.

Woodwork, Hardware, and Glass

Expert guides explain the importance of Galveston and the eleven other battles as they lead visitors through the Capitol. But when they tell them that the ornate woodwork in the building cost only $115,600, there are gasps of disbelief.

The wainscoting alone covers an estimated seven miles. It was made of veneered panels or individual boards to prevent warping and splitting. The woods are native to Texas: oak, pine, cherry, cedar, walnut, ash, and mahogany.

Most of the doors and window frames are of oak and pine. Those in the offices of the governor, the secretary of state, and the original library are of cherry. The ornate reception room and private offices of the governor are trimmed in mahogany. The restrooms and cloakrooms are trimmed in long-leaf yellow pine, while oak is the trim used in most of the other areas.

Skilled craftsmen carved elaborate designs over entrances to offices. Frames for both doors and windows are decorated with designs, many meticulously carved by hand.

Hardware was made to order, at a cost of $90,000 in 1886. Some builders say it would cost $1 million to duplicate it with the same quality.

Original door pulls are of bronze, each with the Lone Star of Texas on the face of the knob and an intricate design on the base. Interestingly, the original door knobs are hollow, being constructed from two half shells seamed together. Each is eighteen inches long. They were cast on the Capitol grounds from designs created by the A. H. Andrews Co. of Chicago.

Door hinges also are of bronze and each original is embellished with the words "TEXAS CAPITOL." The hinges, screws included, weigh over eight pounds each.

Glass for the building is equally ornate. Myers, the architect, wanted to use Belgian glass. Not only was the product beautiful, but the company offered him forty percent of the cost if he could get the contract. The commissioners turned down the proposal and a Massachusetts firm manufactured the glass. However, the American firm supplied only the plain glass used for windows and the three-quarter-inch corrugated skylights that adorned the ceilings of the legislative chambers. The skylights proved unsatisfactory, admitting so much light that it glared on the lawmakers' desks. Later they were covered with paper. When this didn't solve the problem, the lights were painted a green tint to admit light suitable for reading.

For beauty, acid-etched or embossed glass was used in the doors, interior windows, transom lights, and the ceilings of the legislative chambers and library. Some of these pieces, each embossed with the state seal or the Lone Star of Texas, were removed many years ago during a renovation of the building. They are prized collector's items today. This particular glass, made in England, added $29,529.09 to the building's cost, plus $13,684.40 in customs duties.

Cast and Wrought Iron

The convicts who had done most of the labor and much of the stone work on the building also provided some of the cast and wrought iron. Inmates at the East Texas State Penitentiary at Rusk (since converted to the Rusk State Hospital) used the foundry there to cast iron columns. These were used as structural support for the dome, in the legislative halls, and at various other points throughout the building.

Actually, the mushroom-shaped structure that rises 266 feet above the rotunda floor is a double dome. The larger of the two begins at the fifth level 155 feet above the basement floor. Huge columns around the rotunda, each of cast iron and ornamented with zinc, form a base that supports the first, smaller dome. A circular stairway leads from this level between the two domes and emerges on top of the building.

The star on the diaphragm suspended over the center of the inner dome is gold-painted on galvanized steel. The word "T E X A S" is spelled out between the points.

After six years of work, struggle, and triumph, the construction of the Capitol was complete. When the Capitol Syndicate received final title to their land, they had spent $3,744,630. The State assumed approximately $500,000 of that amount. For three million acres of land, valued at $1 per acre, and the $500,000, the State of Texas had built their statehouse.

(ulhp)
Early photo of Capitol office. The original type of wooden shutters can be seen in the background, as well as the familiar wainscoting seen throughout the building. The wainscoting in the Capitol building is of oak, pine, cherry, cedar, walnut, ash, and mahogany and has a combined length of about seven miles. In the original plans, the wainscoting was to have been of marble. This officeholder decorated with posters of attractive young ladies of the day.

(llhp)
Early-day typing pool at the Capitol. When the building was completed in 1888, it housed virtually all of State government in its 392 rooms. Among these were not only the House and Senate, but also offices of the attorney general, governor, treasurer, secretary of state, comptroller, Board of Control, Post Office, Health Department, Labor Bureau, Railroad Commission, and Education Department.

(above)
Turn-of-the-century Capitol office. This was one of the more elaborately furnished offices as indicated by the floral carpeting, chandelier, spittoon, and furniture. In the lower left corner of the photograph is one of the "star back" chairs which were used as original seats for the Texas House of Representatives. The Capitol originally had gas and electric lighting; it was not until March 24, 1891, that the first electric lights shined in the Capitol.

(ulhp)

Photo showing the original encaustic floor tile in one of the Capitol offices. Prior to installation of the present terrazzo floors in 1936, most of the flooring in the public areas was this patterned type of encaustic clay tiling. Other types of floors were wood and glass.

(llhp)

Comptroller's office group portrait taken in 1894 on the steps of the Capitol. John McCall, the state comptroller, is in the middle, bottom row, with the dark mustache.

(above)

Comptroller's Department on the first floor of the Capitol. Notice the reverse lettering on the acid-etched glass transom above the door, which designated the department. Acid-etched glass, used in door and transom panels, contained intricate designs and often the seal of the State of Texas. The glass was imported from England. Gus Wilke, the contractor, paid $13,684 for the 114 cases of glass when it arrived in November 1887. This photograph also shows the ledgers used by the Comptroller's Department (lower left) and the safe (upper left).

(above)
Governor's reception room in 1894. The Victorian influence is evident in the curtains and furniture pictured. The first telephone was installed in the State Capitol in 1887. It was the twenty-fourth phone installed in the city of Austin. The state paid ninety cents a month for telephone service.

(urhp)
Early photograph of the Senate chamber showing the original acid-etched design skylights in the ceiling and the original wooden shutters on the second- and third-floor windows.

(lrhp)
One of the many remodeling efforts in the Capitol. Painters are giving the Senate chamber a new paint job and facelift. One painter is working on the ceiling atop the scaffolding.

(ulhp)
Senate floor activity during the 68th legislative session. Both the "Battle of San Jacinto" and "The Fall of the Alamo" paintings by H. A. McArdle hang in the Senate Chamber. Large composite photo portraits of the Senate members by legislature hang along the chamber floor and gallery walls.

(llhp)
The House of Representatives chamber in 1894. Original furnishings were sparse. The "star back" chairs were used by the legislators and the portraits of Stephen F. Austin on the left and Sam Houston on the right decorated the front of the chamber. In the early years, the House and Senate chambers were often used for dances and receptions.

(below)
Photograph taken about 1920 of the House of Representatives chamber, showing desks and skylights in the ceiling. In 1920 there were 125 members of the House. Redistricting later changed this number to the present 150 members.

House of Representatives
State Capitol, Austin, Texas

Early 1960 photo of the House chamber being used by the Boy Scouts of America. Both chambers have been used to host organizations for mock legislative sessions and meetings. The 1940 voting machine booth and tally boards are evident in this picture. Texas was one of the first governments to use electronic voting, with the installation of its first system in 1922.

(left)

1940 electronic voting board. This voting machine was computerized in 1978 just before the 66th legislative session. While the 150-member Texas House of Representatives has the capability to vote electronically, the 31-member Texas Senate is required to voice vote.

(below)

House floor activity during the 68th legislative session in 1983. The first native Texan to become governor of Texas, James Stephen Hogg (who served 1891–1895), stated: "Teach your children to obey the commands of God, to love good government and struggle to make it better."

The Capitol fence originally cost $22,786. It was made possible by the Board of Fencing and Improving the Capitol Grounds, composed of Governor L. S. Ross, Attorney General J. S. Hogg, and Superintendent of Buildings and Grounds W. P. Hardeman. It was built by Mast, Frost and Company of Springfield, Ohio, and originally had 8,282 five-pointed stars.

The "Buckeye" fence which surrounds the Capitol. The fence was built in Ohio and actually contains the Buckeye design shown in some locations on the fence. The legislature of 1889 appropriated $35,000 to pay for the construction of the fence and it was completed by the Ohio firm in 1890. The iron fence was originally painted black with gold-leaf stars. *(Photo by Mike Fowler)*

Polished granite columns with white Italian marble capitols on the south or main entrance of the statehouse. The architect, E. E. Myers, had originally wanted to use a great deal more marble in the building construction. This may be viewed as a token statement of that effect.

Close-up of bronze Capitol doorknob and faceplate. The original doorknobs are two hollow pieces brazed together. The hardware for the statehouse was made especially for the building by the A. H. Andrews Company of Chicago in 1886, with the Walter Tips Company of Austin acting as the local agent. Note the Lone Star motif.

Close-up of the bronze hinges used throughout the Capitol. The hinges were inscribed "TEXAS CAPITOL" and were made in various sizes to accommodate the different heights of the doors. All of the hardware for the Capitol originally cost the contractor $90,000 in 1886.

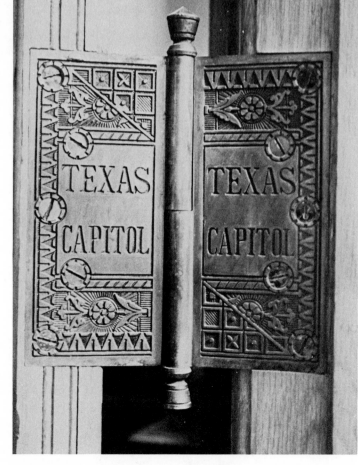

Terrazzo flooring in the rotunda. The terrazzo rotunda floor and other terrazzo flooring was made entirely of native Texas stone, with the exception of the blue stone in the United States seal. The floor was designed by Harold E. Jessen of Austin and constructed by the Art Mosaic and Tile Company of Toledo, Ohio. It was laid in 1936 for the centennial of Texas's independence. The Republic of Texas seal in the center is surrounded by the other five seals of Texas. The original flooring in the rotunda, which is sixty-eight feet in diameter, was partly made of hexagonal glass blocks in a cast-iron frame. The crack in the terrazzo floor is attributed to settling of the building.

(left)
Christmas tree in the hub of the Capitol. Some of these trees were large enough to reach the third floor of the building. The rotunda is used for many ceremonies, events, and displays. It is not uncommon for art and music to be seen, heard, and enjoyed in the rotunda and throughout the Capitol.

(right)
Handcarved oak Texas Seal on the Speaker's podium in the House of Representatives chamber. Many of the various products of Texas are represented in the construction of the Capitol. The wainscoting, for example, is made of native woods; the door and window frames are all of oak or pine.

(left)
Greek-style column in the House chamber. The cast-iron columns in the Capitol draw attention to both their functional strength and ornate beauty. The columns in the House chamber are fluted; other columns are more simple. There are a total of 110 columns inside the Capitol.

(right)
Greek influence inside the Capitol, shown in this detail photograph of plaster work in the rotunda. The plaster work in the Capitol was executed by the firm of Smith and Crimp for $64,200 and completed in May of 1888.

Chandeliers in the House of Representatives chamber. These fixtures have to be lowered with a wench to change the light bulbs. The Senate chamber has an electric wench to lower its chandeliers. These lamps were originally kerosene and later converted to electricity. Electric lights were installed in the Capitol on April 21, 1894. The Capitol built and owned its own 17,000-kilowatt power plant.

(left)
Encaustic tile floor on the fifth level of the rotunda. One of the few places in the Capitol where the original floor is still intact. This level is open for tours through Capitol Security when weather permits and provides a panoramic view of Austin. Tours above this level have been officially closed since 1953. *(Photo by Mike Fowler)*

(below)
Structural steel and metal sheathing between the two domes of the Capitol. This area, still with its original paint job, provides an interesting architectural insight into the building. *(Photo by Ron Whitfield)*

The star, eight feet in diameter, at the top of the suspended dome. Made of sheet metal, the star spells out TEXAS on its points. This was not originally installed in the Capitol, but was done at a later date. It is 309 feet 8 inches from the grade line of the building to its top. (*Photo by Tom McCormick*)

The beauty of the inner dome of the rotunda reflected in its magnificent detail. The dome within a dome is illustrated by the spiral staircase centered in this photo, which travels from the fifth level to between the domes and on to the top of the Capitol.

The stairs that go above the diaphragm suspended above the inner dome. There is a viewing area at the top of these stairs. An interesting Capitol fact is that from the basement to the very top of the Capitol dome there are exactly 500 stair steps. *(Photo by Tom McCormick)*

(next two pages)
"Little Campus — Big Town," watercolor by Mary Doerr, depicts the renovated "little campus" area with neoclassical structures contsructed by Abner Cook.
to the very top of the Capitol dome there are exactly 500

The Capitol Story
Part IV

16

Some Little-Known Stories About a Well-Known Building

In the century since Texas moved its government into the pink granite building in Austin, the place has been used for everything from a concert hall to a brothel. It has been used as a hotel, a dancehall, and the set for a movie, among other things.

Since its dedication, the Capitol has been both the headquarters of the state government and a residence. Behind the House of Representatives chamber, a large apartment furnishes living quarters for the Speaker. In the east wing, off the Senate chamber, there are similar accommodations for the lieutenant governor. In recent years, however, both apartments have been used for entertaining and for additional offices and not as residences.

The governor has only the ornate reception room that adjoins his office for ceremonial events and entertaining. His residence is a block away in the Executive Mansion that has been the official home of chief executives since 1856.

Planners never intended for the Capitol to be used as a residence. In fact, a law adopted at the time specifically prohibited the use of any part of the building as a bedroom. Originally, the area now used by the lieutenant governor for entertaining was the Supreme Court chamber. The west wing area, once the home of the Speaker of the House when he was in town, formerly was office space.

The custom of residential use of the Capitol evolved slowly. Apartments for the two elected officials did not exist until after the turn of the century. Apparently, it was the late Sam Rayburn, when he was Speaker of the Texas House before going on to hold the same post in Congress, who initiated the practice.

The legislature did not repeal the law prohibiting bedrooms in the Capitol until 1943. However,

as late as 1957, one senator tried to get Lieutenant Governor Ben Ramsey and Speaker Waggoner Carr ousted from their quarters. He claimed that the free rent represented additional compensation for the two officals and was unconstitutional. He did not succeed in evicting them.

Costs of the apartment staffs are paid by the state. The amount of domestic help varies with the use the two officers make of the conveniences. In some cases, both officers have preferred to maintain their own residences in Austin, using the apartments only for entertaining and use by special guests.

Living in the Capitol has not been restricted to these two officers of the government, however. In 1891, the *Austin American-Statesman* complained in its January 29 issue with this headline and story:

The Magnificent Texas Capitol
Put to an Undignified Use

The Capitol of Texas appears to have turned into a cheap John lodging house . . . It is quite evident that it should be so called for there are many members and officers of the Legislature now rooming there in different offices, corridors, garrets and in any corner where they can find room for a cot.

The paper went on to suggest that the legislators promptly find other lodgings since "the $5 a day paid to members is to pay their expenses at legitimate boardinghouses and hotels."

Temporary use of the Capitol as a hotel has all but disappeared in recent years, although weary legislators sometimes still catch a few hours of rest in their offices after working late into the night. They are paid a bit more these days, receiving $600 a month whether in session or not. They also get an additional $30 a day for expenses when they are meeting, so most feel that they can afford public lodging.

Ladies and Gentlemen of the Press

So far as the record shows, reporters and television cameramen have never used the Capitol as a hotel. A great many have napped there, however, as they listened to hours of dull oratory and even more lethargic sessions of House and Senate committees.

Those who planned the Capitol were very much aware of the power and the importance of the press and made proper provision for members of the Fourth Estate. The new Capitol had not one, but two, press rooms — each sixteen by thirty-six feet. To make sure that neither legislative body was favored in the headlines, the press rooms were placed in either wing just outside the House and Senate chambers.

Being the good politicians that they were and anxious to keep the writing fraternity happy, legislators provided some amenities unique for the times. Each press room was equipped not only with its own toilet but also with the best quality brass spitoons that the Furnishing Board could supply.

There was only one problem: The reporters didn't use the facilities. In fact, newspaper publishers apparently thought the activities of state government were so unimportant that not one reporter was assigned to cover the Capitol in the early years. Capitol historian Bill Green says it probably was in the 1920s before reporters were assigned to any kind of regular situation where they would have working space provided.

Today the single press room overflows with representatives of the press, radio, and television. Beginning in 1984, some lawmakers have argued that the press should be ousted and their working quarters converted for government functions.

Of Prostitutes and Movies About Them

Although sex escapades have been associated with politics and politicians since biblical times, only the Texas Capitol has been charged in recent years with housing a brothel under its dome.

Again it was the *Austin American-Statesman*, the traditional journalistic watchdog over Texas political shenanigans, that published a 1970 story about how a group of young women were using their weekends to sell sex at the Capitol. It seems that one enterprising lady of the evening, aware that the big build-

ing welcomed visitors around the clock, decided that it was an ideal spot to do some entertaining for pay.

Her invitation list apparently was limited to young men from the Gary Job Corps Center in San Marcos, who poured into Austin each weekend for rest and recreation. The woman and her colleagues arranged trysts with them in the Capitol. There, while one of the women acted as lookout, the others entertained their paying guests in the secluded nooks that dot the long corridors in the building.

The entrepreneurs finally were spotted by Capitol guards. However, nobody could be found who was willing to file charges and the matter was dropped. Now it is remembered only as a footnote to the building's exciting history.

Although there was no direct connection between the fourth-floor brothel operation at the Capitol and the now famed Chicken Ranch at LaGrange in Fayette County, the old building was to have a major role in memorializing the pay-for-play bordello. For the first time in its history, the Capitol was transformed into a movie set for the production of a musical called *The Best Little Whorehouse in Texas*.

Motion pictures had been made around the Capitol before, and interior shots have been edited into final productions. This time, however, the Capitol itself, and especially its beautiful rotunda, had a featured role. It served as one of the actual sets for the filming of the story of the Chicken Ranch, the oldest continuously operating brothel in America when it was closed August 2, 1973. In fact, the Chicken Ranch antedated the Capitol by almost a half century.

The famous old brothel operated until the revelations of a Houston television reporter forced its closing. A large number of Central Texans objected, but eventually the governor, the attorney general, and the Texas Rangers prevailed and the Chicken Ranch was padlocked. It was then that a Texas writer, Larry King, decided the place deserved at least a footnote to history and wrote *The Best Little Whorehouse in Texas* as a Broadway play.

The hit play was converted into a motion picture in the 1980s. The star was Burt Reynolds, who played the role of the Fayette County sheriff who was reluctant to shut down one of his area's best-known attractions. Country-western star Dolly Parton had the role of Miss Mona Reynolds (a fictional name), the bordello's madam. Charles Durning played the governor of Texas, and one of the memorable scenes of the movie was his jumping behind the columns of the Capitol's second-floor rotunda as he sang "I Love to Do the Sidestep."

The Best Little Whorehouse hasn't led to the Capitol being converted into a motion picture studio. At least, not yet.

Never Bashful About Using Their Capitol

Texans didn't object to the use of their Capitol as a movie set, even if prostitution was the subject of the production. The citizens always have regarded the building as an auditorium for the use of the people. Thousands of them have spent long hours working, celebrating, laughing, and crying inside its halls. In fact, the Capitol has always been more of a monument to the aspirations of the people than a mere statehouse.

As a result, they have made good use of their investment. It has been the scene of weddings, wakes, funerals, dances, galas, parties, and meetings of every kind. Before the turn of the century, it was not unusual for the legislature to clear its chambers, removing the desks when necessary, to accommodate a variety of events.

The Capitol was less than a year old when Lawrence Sullivan Ross, who as governor had presided at the Capitol's dedication, chose to take the oath for his second term in the House of Representatives on January 15, 1889. Many other governors followed his lead. In 1947, Beauford Jester was sworn into the office on the building's front steps, but he had the desks removed from the Senate chamber for his inaugural ball that evening.

For the most part, in recent years, the business of government has increased so much that the Capitol no longer can accommodate the kind of affairs it once hosted to the delight of Texans. There are still receptions in the rotunda, in the private apartments, and in the governor's reception room. But the galas of another day are a part of history. An exception to this was the recent black tie dinner and extravaganza held in its corridors during the centennial celebration.

Most of the activities that draw visitors to the public rooms today take place in the House or Senate chambers when these bodies are in session. It is in these rooms that dreams and schemes are perpetrated, proposals are debated, and plans perfected. Sometimes these activities are punctuated with bitter arguments and even an occasional fistfight.

Often these events make colorful headlines. On February 21, 1933, the *Dallas Morning News* carried a banner story: "Senator Hits Lawyer with Heavy Pitcher after Lie Is Passed." Sometimes these disagreements can't be settled orally or with the heaving of a piece of pottery. They are resolved in the corridor more emphatically.

Assassination

Arguments and fights in the Capitol, sometimes on the floor of the Senate or House, are not unusual. However, there also have been two murders. In the first incident, robbery, not political revenge, was the motive. It happened on the entrance steps and not inside the building.

The events leading up to the shooting began on February 19, 1873, at the Old Stone Capitol when Representative Louis Francke of Fayette County stopped by the office of the House Sergeant-at-Arms. He wanted to pick up his per diem and travel reimbursement. The legislature was in recess and was nearing adjournment, so Francke walked down Congress Avenue to have a beer.

He paid for his drink with a large bill, then lingered awhile before returning to the Capitol about 7:00 P.M. There he was attacked by two men who apparently had seen him pocket the change from his purchase of the beer and had been lying in wait for him. They accosted him as he walked up the steps to the main entrance, beat him about the head with a rock, took his wallet, and tossed him down the entry. He died a few hours later. Although a number of witnesses noticed the two strangers on the steps and a nearby grocer remembered selling them some beer, the murderers were never apprehended.

The only other murder, apparently a planned assassination, happened in a Capitol office on a June morning in 1903.

A former employee dropped in to see his ex-boss, Comptroller R. M. Love. So far as it was known, there was no animosity between them. They appeared to be chatting easily when the visitor suddenly pulled out a gun and shot Love. An assistant grappled with the assailant and the pistol discharged again, this time into his stomach. He died a few minutes later on the first floor of the south corridor. Comptroller Love was rushed to a hospital, but he also died later that day.

Fire!

Having lost two of their four capitols in Austin to fire, Texans were hopeful that the granite monument they erected to their government in 1888 would be impervious to flame. It isn't.

On January 25, 1988, the Capitol Preservation Board was warned that the building is a fire hazard. This came as no surprise. Five years before, a tragic fire on the second floor killed one and threatened to engulf the entire building.

It happened in the early morning of February 6, 1983. Katherine Hobby, the eighteen-year-old daughter of Lieutenant Governor Bill Hobby, and three of her friends were spending the night in Hobby's Capitol apartment. Apparently, an electrical short in an outlet in the den was the origin of the blaze.

One of the guests, twenty-three-year-old Matthew Hansen of New Caney, died of smoke inhalation. Miss Hobby and the other guests escaped unharmed, but three firemen and a Capitol policeman were hospitalized with injuries. Another officer and two other firemen had to be treated for minor burns and bruises.

Fortunately, only the apartment was seriously damaged. But Austin's acting fire chief, Brady Pool, said he feared for two hours that the entire Capitol would be destroyed.

The danger still exists five years after the tragic fire. The imposing granite walls of the century-old structure actually mask the real vulnerability to flame. The building has numerous elevator shafts and stairways that act like chimneys and it is full of woodwork and false ceilings.

The superstructure is fireproof, consisting of brick vaults over steel beams five feet apart and a granite exterior. But experts say that many electrical transformers are in poor condition and that the entire building needs to be rewired. Only the basement is equipped with automatic sprinklers. Other areas depend on automatic smoke detectors and the Capitol Police.

Water lines in the building are deteriorating, and heating, air-conditioning, and ventilating systems also need replacing. In fact, an overhaul that would cost many more millions than Texans paid for their original Capitol appears a future necessity.

If and when that will come is a decision that rests with the Capitol Preservation Board. Members are trying to find a solution as the building which Temple Houston predicted "will stand through all eternity" begins its second century.

Security Today

Although the efficient Capitol Police could not prevent the tragic 1983 fire and may be unable to prevent another, the building today is protected round-the-clock. Modern electronic devices and a highly trained police force protect the building and those who work there.

Its most unique sentries, however, and the ones who have the most contact with visitors are the unarmed men known simply as "car guards." Many of these men are retirees who are seventy and older. Their principal assignment is to keep tourists and other visitors away from the parking places reserved for state officials and legislators. They pass their days whittling, talking with visitors, and feeding the dozens of squirrels and hundreds of grackles that swarm the grounds as they keep an ever-watchful eye on those prized parking spaces.

"It's the only job where you can sit under a shade tree all day and talk with somebody for two hours and not feel guilty about doing your job," one car guard said.

They are instructed to be polite, but firm, with visitors. If someone still insists on taking a reserved parking space, the guard says nothing, waits until the visitor has gone inside, and then calls the Capitol Police. The police may issue a ticket or, in some cases, may have the offending vehicle towed away. But they do it with a smile!

(above)
Capitol view of downtown Austin taken in the early 1890s. The temporary Capitol which burned in 1899 still stands in this photo. The limestone county courthouse stands out across the street.

(below)
Northwest view from the Capitol shows the Balcones Fault Line on the horizon. This geological fault goes all the way from Mexico to Oklahoma. Some very fine Victorian homes are evident in this photograph.

(above)

1888 picture of the Governor's Mansion from the new Capitol. Note the gazebo on the Governor's Mansion grounds and the white horse and its buggy hitched outside of the mansion. The Governor's Mansion is older than the present Capitol building. Contracted in 1854, it was designed by Abner Cook and constructed in 1855 and 1856. In June 1856, Governor Pease became the first occupant of the mansion. Its appropriated cost was $14,500, with an additional $2,500 for furnishings.

(below)
1888 photograph taken from the Colorado River bridge looking north to the new Capitol. Evidence of a frontier atmosphere still exists.

(ulhp)
1888 photograph taken from a point west of the Capitol provides an interesting angle. Horses and a wagon await at the west doors of the building. It is said that the basement of the Capitol was used as a stable during inclement weather in the early days of the building's use. The Capitol covers three acres of ground and has eighteen acres of floor space. When it was completed in 1888, the building was said to be the seventh largest building in the world.

(above)
Congress Avenue looking north to the Capitol. The spired building next to Patterson Wagon Yard was the old railroad depot built in 1888. The lines used for the trolley and horses and wagons are evident on Congress Avenue. Austin at this date was the western terminus of the Southern Pacific and on the route of the International and Great Northern Railroad.

(ulhp)
1889 picture of the State Capitol as seen through a German Glee Club archway built on Congress Avenue. Tracks for streetcars or "trolleys" are visible in the photograph. In 1889 these streetcars were run by electricity. The city had fifteen miles of street railways.

(llhp)
The Capitol is complete and stands mighty on the Austin skyline. The Colorado River is visible in the middle of this photograph. To the north of the Capitol is University Hill. In 1889 tuition was free at the newly created State University.

(this page)
Early photo (circa 1889) of the completed Capitol, taken from the temporary Capitol building. Notice the large United States flag flying over the south pediment and the telegraph lines in the foreground. The drive around the building has been completed.

F. Teich, Builder, San Antonio, Tex.

(ulhp)
This photo of the Capitol, taken from the southwest, clearly shows the "Buckeye" fence around the 25.96 acres of Capitol grounds. The fence was completed in 1890 and made possible by the Board for Fencing and Improving the Capitol Grounds.

(llhp)
Magnificent she stands, the Texas Statehouse photographed on August 3, 1891. Here the Capitol drive is in place and landscaping has been started. In the right corner of the photo a visitor carries an umbrella to provide shade from the hot summer sun. The smokestack at upper right was an energy plant for the Capitol.

(this page)
The Confederate monument on the Capitol grounds, photographed shortly after it was placed in 1901. Frank Teich of San Antonio was the sculptor and builder. Jefferson Davis is the figure on top; the other four men represent the cavalry, infantry, artillery, and navy.

(ulhp)
The Capitol after the Buckeye fence was erected around the grounds. This photo shows the Capitol gates, which have since been removed and placed at the State Cemetery.

(llhp)
Early twentieth-century snowfall at the State Capitol blankets the grounds.

(this page)
1901 photograph taken at the dedication of the Confederate Heroes Monument, placed in honor of those who died serving the Confederacy. The county courthouse is the building at right.

(ulhp)
Arch of welcome erected to honor President McKinley's visit on May 3, 1901. The Capitol has hosted presidents, foreign heads of state, and dignitaries too numerous to mention. Austin went to great lengths to honor President McKinley. Four months after his visit to Austin, the president was assassinated in New York by Leon Czolgosz.

(llhp)
1901 photograph of Texans turning out for President William McKinley's visit. This picture, taken from the east or Senate side of Capitol Park, shows the styles of the day and gives a classic view of the "Buckeye" fence.

(below)
Turn-of-the-century Congress Avenue, with Scarbrough and Hicks Department Store on the west side of the street. Traffic abounds and business appears to be brisk. Note moonlight tower to the left of the Capitol. By 1895, thirty-two of these towers had been constructed in Austin.

(this page)
1905 photograph of Congress Avenue and the Capitol. Still in the horse and buggy days, downtown is bustling with activity. The wagon of George Wesley, a tailor, is hitched at lower left.

(urhp)
1910 photograph from the southeast, showing the Capitol with horses and carriages in the drive. The grounds have recently been landscaped in this picture. Notice the granite shaft at right. Later that year, a bronze of a Confederate soldier sculpted by Pompeo Coppini was placed atop as a monument to members of Hood's Brigade.

(lrhp)
Austin in transition on Congress Avenue in the 1910s. A parade progresses down the avenue, along with horses and buggies and early-vintage automobiles. In 1907 legislation was passed requiring that automobiles be licensed at a cost of fifty cents in the county where they were owned. Automobile owners were required to make their own license plates until the first uniform state license plates were made in 1917.

141

1913 Main streetcar photograph showing Congress Avenue and Sixth Street. Progress has brought the electrified street-car to Austin and "skyscrapers" flank the street.

Stately photograph of the Capitol, taken from the southeast part of the grounds. The Doric aspects of Greek architecture are seen throughout the Capitol building. In early days at the Capitol grounds, horses and cows often grazed at will and buggies parked where their drivers wished.

(above)
Dedication of the original Fireman's monument on July 7, 1896, with a crowd of about 500 in attendance. This monument was replaced in 1905 with a bronze, nine-foot-tall fireman holding a child and a lantern.

(urhp)
1907 photograph of workmen lowering Terry's Texas Ranger statue into place. Pompeo Coppini's work is placed on a granite base.

(lrhp)
Interesting photo of the Capitol, taken from a location northeast of the building. At this time, the gentleman in the foreground was probably out in the country surrounding Austin.

145

(above)
Two horse-drawn wagons move along Eleventh Street in front of the Capitol. The trees are beginning to grow tall along the front walk. A Texas flag flies over the building.

(urhp)
Armistice Day Parade on November 11, 1918, ending World War I. Flags and five thousand soldiers from The University of Texas military schools are plentiful at this crowded event. During World War I, the names of American soldiers from Texas killed in action were announced from the south steps of the Capitol.

(lrhp)
1926 photograph of a paved Congress Avenue lined with parked cars.

Early aerial photograph of Austin and the Capitol. An interesting story about the statehouse is that until 1925 it was technically owned by two sisters, Mrs. Kate Sturgis and Mrs. Stella MacDonald. Their father, Gen. T. S. Chambers, had transferred title to his daughters for the land on which the Capitol stands. In 1925 the legislature finally agreed to pay the sisters $25,000 for the land, and they deeded the Capitol grounds to the State of Texas.

1920s photograph of Austin shows the brick-paved avenue and automobiles lining the street. Large American flags fly over the Scarbrough and Littlefield buildings. Economic good times had set in following World War I.

Austin Street Railway Company Streetcar #26 on Colorado Street, west of the Capitol. Photographs such as this indicate the character of the city in many ways. The driveways around the Capitol were properly curbed and paved in 1912 at a cost of $25,000.

A tornado as it twisted over the Capitol and Austin at 4:15 P.M. on May 4, 1922, killing twelve people and injuring fifty more. This extremely rare photograph alludes to the approximately half a million dollars in property damage which was reported.

Capitol staircase. The cast-iron work in the grand staircases of the Capitol were imported from Belgium. Staircases were designed as the primary means of getting from floor to floor in the Capitol. In addition to the stairs, there were also two original Otis elevators installed in 1886. There were water hydraulics, with the storage tanks kept in the fifth-level attic and the artesian well as the water source. *(Photo by Ron Whitfield)*

Beautifully decorated in period Victorian furnishings, the governor's reception room is photographed as it is today. This office is used for guests, official business, press conferences, signing of legislation, and other ceremonial functions. It is the only room in the Capitol to have cherrywood for the wainscoting and woodwork. *(Photo by Ron Whitfield)*

The Senate chamber after its renovation in 1983. The Senate restored the chamber with wooden shutters for the windows, reproductions of the original skylights, new patterned carpeting, and a general facelift following the tragic fire of early February 1983.

Recent color photograph of the House of Representatives chamber. The chamber is 96 by 100 feet and has a public gallery which seats over 500 people. The framed flag between the United States and Texas flags is the original San Jacinto battle flag known as the "Pride of the House." *(Photo by Ron Whitfield)*

Roof of the Capitol. The roof of the Capitol is of fourteen-ounce copper covering 85,000 square feet, with locked seams and all the joints soldered together. At the May 18, 1888, dedication ceremony, the roof leaked and still does. A 1937 Senate Committee Report mentioned that "there are several hundred leaks in the roof, and it stands in need of immediate repair . . . The condition of the dome is extremely bad." *(Photo by Ron Whitfield)*

Fifth-level columns of the Capitol made of cast iron painted to resemble granite. Basically, the entire outer shell of the Capitol above the roof line is made of metal. In January of 1887, it was decided that the inner dome walls would be of brick construction to the level of the colonnade ceiling in the dome and that a system of tie rods, beams, and braces would be used to strengthen the dome and lantern. *(Photo by Ron Whitfield)*

Spiral staircase going from the fifth level to between the double domes of the Capitol. The Texas Capitol is one of only three major buildings in the world to have such a double dome. The other two are the Basilica (St. Peter's) in Rome and St. Paul's in London. *(Photo by Tom McCormick)*

The inner Capitol dome as seen from the rotunda. It is 266 feet from the star in the Texas seal on the first floor to the star on the top of the dome. A tragic accident occurred on February 20, 1922, when Edwin Wheeler, a painter working on the rotunda, fell to his death. It is said that a small hook that held the scaffolding next to the fifth-floor rotunda wall straightened out and allowed the rope to come loose. Wheeler had just stood up and gone over to see why the rope was slipping. His head hit the wall, causing him to be flung outward. He hit the railing and fell to the glass floor, shattering it and crashing to the basement. *(Photo by Ron Whitfield)*

(preceding page)
Shrouded in green scaffolding, the goddess makes ready for descent from her perch on the rainy morning of November 24, 1985. *(Photo by Ron Whitfield)*

(this page)
A Texas National Guard CH-47 makes an unsuccessful attempt to put the Goddess of Liberty II atop the Capitol in 1986. *(Photo by Ron Whitfield)*

(next page)
The dome of the Capitol stands out in the darkness of night. The lighted Lone Star atop the Capitol was temporarily placed there by City of Austin electric department workers to shine over the city during most of the time that the Capitol was without a Goddess. *(Photo by Ron Whitfield)*

On a beautiful day, the new Goddess II takes her place atop the Capitol with the assistance of a Mississippi National Guard CH-54 "Skycrane" helicopter on June 14, 1986. *(Photo by Ron Whitfield)*

Happy birthday, Capitol! 100 ten-foot-tall candles surround the capitol building's dome during the early morning prior to the Centennial celebration. The Heritage Society of Austin was responsible for coordinating the construction of the candles. *(Photo by Mike Fowler)*

(above)
Aerial photo of the Capitol area looking down Congress Avenue toward Town Lake. The growth of the downtown area has been phenomenal, yet amongst this build-up, the acreage around the Capitol provides an oasis for Austin.

(right)
Bluebonnets, the state flower, provide the foreground of spring for the Capitol. This photo was taken from northeast of the Capitol. *(Photo by Reagan Bradshaw)*

The entire skyline is lit up with lightning bolts in this photograph of Austin, The University of Texas Tower, and the Texas Capitol dome. *(Photo by Reagan Bradshaw)*

Storm clouds brew over the Capitol. Buildings on The University of Texas campus and state office buildings fill the skyline north of the Capitol.

Splendid snow scene of the Capitol taken in 1985 from the southwest part of the grounds.
(Photo by Barbara Schlief)

Christmas lights over Congress Avenue create a splash of color and activity in this Capitol photograph.

Evening falls on the Capitol, displaying a serene majesty over the Austin horizon. *(Photo by Barbara Schlief)*

(lhp)
Spectacular fireworks explode around the lighted capitol on July 4, 1984. Photo taken from South Austin. *(Photo by Gale Kloesel)*

(this page)
The magnificent sunrise captures the beauty of two domed buildings. In the early 1900s someone remarking on the greatness of the Capitol said: "It was built by giants but now it's inhabited by pygmies." Our challenge for the future is to preserve its grandeur.

Amid the boom in downtown construction, the Capitol is still visible from Congress Avenue in this 1985 photograph taken from Fourth Street. *(Photo by Ron Whitfield)*

Photograph taken in June 1987 from directly in front of the Capitol building on Congress Avenue shows that beautiful pictures, as in the past, can still be found. New trees have been planted along the great walk to the south of our statehouse. *(Photo by Ron Whitfield)*

Aerial photograph taken prior to 1924, showing much of old Austin. The old county courthouse (bottom middle), the original General Land Office (lower middle left), and Memorial Stadium on The University of Texas campus (upper middle) are seen in this picture. The first Capitol renovation since its completion in 1888 was done in 1928, with about $1 million being spent on the facelift.

Snow scene on the Capitol grounds in 1929, showing the serene quality which the building is capable of assuming. Perhaps this winter snowstorm was a signal of the coming Depression that swept the nation.

(above)
Capitol building and its grounds gripped by ice and snow in 1929. Then, as now, the city came to a virtual standstill until the weather subsided. The Capitol was heated by steam piped in from a boiler house east of the building, which was connected to the Capitol by a tunnel.

(left)
A 1929 snowstorm turned the Capitol grounds into a winter wonderland.

CONGRESS AVENUE FROM
SOUTH AUSTIN JUNE, 15·1935

(ulhp)
These wagons, stopped near the Governor's Mansion, belong to a group of Texas farmers protesting farming conditions in the 1930s.

(llhp)
The Great Flood of 1935 took place on June 15, when the Colorado River completely left its banks and did enormous damage to Austin. The Capitol was safe, sitting high upon her hill. Notice above the water the sign for "State House Coffee." This was an Austin-based company that manufactured food staples such as spices, teas, and coffee.

(this page)
A striking view of the State Capitol, taken through The University of Texas Tower clock before the workings of the clock were installed. This photograph was taken in 1936, one hundred years after Texas won her freedom.

155

1940s photograph showing the Texas Capitol standing tall. Only one other domed capitol in the United States is taller, that being the Illinois State Capitol at 405 feet in height. The Capitol of Texas is the largest example of renaissance revival architecture in the United States.

The State Capitol in the 1940s as it majestically fills the skyline.

Early aerial photo of the Capitol. This photo illustrates that the Capitol building is built in the form of a Greek cross, with protruding flanks and a dome and rotunda at the intersection of the main corridors. The building is 566 feet and 6 inches long, 288 feet and 10 inches wide. At the time of dedication, the building had 392 rooms, 18 vaults, 924 windows, and 404 doors.

A 1949 snow scene shows more of the beauty that the elements can bestow on the Texas State Capitol.

1950s panorama of downtown Austin, taken across Town Lake from South Congress. On a billboard at left, Will Wilson is seeking election to a statewide office.

(left)
A misty mood envelops the Capitol. This view is often seen by those who work the long hours required during a legislative session.

(below)
A full moon illuminates the domed building for this night exposure.

A cloudy day creates a feeling of stately strength for this mighty structure.

(above)
1950s Christmas on Congress Avenue. The lights were strung along the entirety of the avenue, creating a festive and colorful pageant for the Capitol to oversee.

(left)
A full moon shines down on a lighted dome, and the Capitol points to the heavens.

An unusual aerial view of the State Capitol taken in 1954 shows the fine construction and architectural aspects of the building.

(below)
Scene taken from the front door of the main building at The University of Texas, which provides a nice frame for the statehouse.

(above)
Removal of the mammoth lighted star in May of 1969 by order of the legislature.

(above)
A workman sandblasting the Goddess of Liberty on May 22, 1969.

(upper right)
The United States invasion of Cambodia draws a large protest crowd on The University of Texas campus in 1970. The State Capitol, symbol of authority, looms in the background.

(lower right)
1971 graduates of The University of Texas attend commencement exercises at the Main Mall, with the Capitol in the background.

(above)
An estimated $85,000 of damage was done to the trees on the Capitol grounds by a violent windstorm in August of 1972. It was reported in the *Austin American-Statesman* that "The park-like area still looks like a battlefield. Most of the giant trees felled by the wind lie where they were blown down . . . Only the trunks of some trees remain upright, with their great limbs splintered and twisted to the ground like broken umbrellas."

(left)
An early morning mist awakens the Capitol and its new neighbors on the skyline.

(rhp)
Ice on the tree branches produces a magical image for the luminated dome in this picture taken in January of 1978.

Texas flags abound on Congress Avenue in this photograph
taken from Third Street in the 1980s.

Night photograph taken on July 22, 1982, showing the lighted Capitol dome's reflection on the rain-wet asphalt of Congress Avenue.

(below)
Annual Christmas caroling in the rotunda of the State Capitol. This 1980s photograph is taken from the fourth level, looking down on top of the Capitol Christmas tree.

17

The Capitol and
The Next Hundred Years

In the last decade of its first century of existence, the magnificent Capitol of Texas lost a battle its planners hoped would never be fought. Real estate development in the central city overcame the objections of the people and dwarfed the view of the beautiful old building with high-rises of stone and glass.

The pink granite Capitol dome once loomed over panoramic views from historic locations: Mount Bonnell in west Austin, the Garden Center in Zilker Park, St. Edwards University, and a dozen other sites. Even after the construction of Interstate 35 through the city's heart in the 1950s, travelers entering Austin on this expressway from either the north or south were treated to a magnificent picture of the state's seat of government.

For a period, the Austin City Planning Commission hoped to keep it that way. Their goal was to follow the lead of Washington, D.C., and limit the height of all downtown structures so the Capitol would always be the dominant building. Twice the commission's proposed ordinance was rejected by the City Council, however, and Congress Avenue and adjoining streets have become a jungle of skyscrapers.

The problem really began years before when the state government started the building revolution. In June 1933, the Department of Highways and Public Transportation Building was completed at Eleventh and Congress, directly across from the Capitol. This started a rash of new multistoried government buildings that threatened to engulf the majestic Capitol on three sides.

Taking a cue from the state's rush to fill up the Capitol complex with offices, Austin developers got into the act. In 1961, despite the objections of Governor Price Daniel and members of the legislature, the City Council approved construction of a twenty-

four-story apartment high-rise immediately west of the Capitol. That started a rash of skyscraper hotels and office buildings that continues unabated. As a result, the center of Congress Avenue is about the only place where one can get an unobstructed glimpse of at least the front of the Capitol.

Preserving What's Left

Although the panoramic view of the beautiful old building is gone forever, an effort—albeit a late one—is being made to renovate and restore the Capitol to its original basic integrity. As befitting a building that was made a National Historic Landmark by the U.S. Department of the Interior in 1987—one of only eighteen other structures in the country to be so honored—the Capitol has a new lease on life. A Preservation Board headed by the governor and lieutenant governor has been appointed, a resident architect employed, and a committee of prominent citizens named to raise funds for the project.

The precedent for such a move was set in the late 1970s and early 1980s, when Texans finally got around to renovating the home of their chief executive. The Governor's Mansion, built in 1856 for $17,000, had been in use for thirty-two years when the present Capitol was completed. By that time, some felt that it should be replaced since a new statehouse was in the offing. A proposal to do just that was made in 1886.

The Mansion survived that onslaught, but calls for a new residence for the governor were made again in 1918 and in 1936. John Connally, during his term as governor in the 1960s, asked the legislature for funds for a new Mansion and suggested that the old one on a hill just east of the Capitol should become a state museum.

None of these proposals came to fruition, and each governor and his family continued to make improvements to the old building as budgets permitted. Then, in 1979, Governor William P. Clements, Jr., got the legislature to appropriate $1 million to renovate the residence. After two years and the eventual expenditure of some $3 million in state funds and private donations, the Executive Mansion emerged as one of the nation's finest.

Probably nothing would have been done about the Capitol itself, however, if the tragic fire had not occurred in the apartment of the lieutenant governor. The legislature responded by appropriating $6 million to repair the damage to the Capitol and set up the State Preservation Board to plan and execute a long-range program of renovation and restoration.

In 1987 the legislature approved the issuance of up to $67.5 million in revenue bonds to finance the Preservation Board's work on the century-old structure. Private donations also will be sought as the plans materialize.

A Final Word

In the century and more since couples parked their buggies on what was then called "Kissing Hill," the Capitol complex has become clogged with automobiles. The building itself, designed to house all branches of government in perpetuity, long ago became outmoded with demands for government services in this second century. Solving these problems, and restoring the building to its original nineteenth-century magnificence, are the challenges that the Preservation Board and the people of Texas will face over the years to come.

That the challenges will be met and the Capitol preserved for generations yet unborn is a certainty. When Texans gathered in Austin in May 1988 to celebrate the Capitol's centennial, much work already had been done. The governor's reception room, often called the "Living Room of Texas," had been largely restored. The chamber of the House of Representatives was beginning to look the way it did around the turn of the century.

The new carpet would be especially pleasing to the late president of the United States, Lyndon B. Johnson. He never served in the Texas legislature, but his father, Sam Johnson, did. And Sam Johnson had a subtle role in selecting the new floor covering.

In trying to determine the style of carpeting used in the House in early years, Capitol curator Bonnie Campbell found a 1905 photograph of Representative Sam Johnson. The photo of Johnson seated at his Capitol desk showed the carpet pattern in detail. As a result, it was possible to reproduce the old carpeting exactly.

Texans in 1988, like Temple Houston in his 1888 dedicatory speech, agree that "the architecture of a civilization is its most enduring feature." They want to make sure, as Houston predicted, that their Capitol truly "shall stand as a sentinel of eternity."

The Capitol has had more than her share of tragedy under her dome. In February 1983 a tragic fire broke out in the lieutenant governor's apartment, killing a young guest by smoke inhalation. In September 1977 a mental patient leaped from the third floor of the rotunda and died from injuries. A painter accidentally fell to his death while working on the inner dome in 1922. In 1903 the state comptroller, R. M. Love, was murdered on the first floor of the Capitol by a former employee. An assistant grappled with the assailant and the murderer was killed by his own gun, thus two people died that day.

(right)
Fire engine outside the Senate wing of the Capitol in February of 1983. Considerable damage was done, and one young man was killed in the blaze.

(below)
Water and smoke damage in the first floor east wing of the Capitol, resulting from the 1983 fire.

(this page)
The State Capitol stands tall and mighty on the Austin horizon in the 1880s.

(urhp)
1974 photograph taken from the American Bank Tower. Many views of the Capitol have already been blocked.

(lrhp)
1890s photograph of the Austin skyline. Notice the artificial moonlight towers scattered over the horizon.

Bibliography

Allen, Ruth Alice. "The Capitol Boycott: A Study in Peaceful Labor Tactics." *Southwestern Historical Quarterly* 42, no. 4 (April 1939).

Andrus, M. Walter. *Behind This Cornerstone*. Austin: Chapman Printing Co., 1956.

Barker, Eugene C. *The Life of Stephen F. Austin*. Austin: University of Texas Press, 1969.

Barkley, Mary Starr. *A History of Central Texas*. Austin: Austin Printing Co., 1970.

Bateman, Audray, and Katherine Hart. *Waterloo Scrapbook: 1972–1976*. Austin: Friends of the Public Library, 1976.

———. *A History of Travis County and Austin, 1839–1899*. Waco: Texian Press, 1963.

Berry, Margaret C. *The University of Texas: A Pictorial Account of Its First Century*. Austin and London: University of Texas Press, 1980.

Blythe, T. Roger. *Capitols of the United States of America*. Tucson, Arizona: 1963.

Clark, Sara. *The Capitols of Texas: A Visual History*. Austin: Encino Press, 1975.

Clarke, Mary Whatley. *David G. Burnet*. Austin and New York: Pemberton Press, 1969.

Connor, Seymour V. et al. *Capitols of Texas*. Waco: Texian Press, 1970.

Daniel, Jean Houston, Price Daniel, and Dorothy Blodgett. *The Texas Governor's Mansion*. Austin: Texas State Library and Archives Commission and Liberty: Sam Houston Regional Library and Research Center, 1984.

Duke, Cordia Sloan, and Joe B. Frantz. *6,000 Miles of Fence: Life on the XIT Ranch of Texas*. Austin: University of Texas Press, 1961.

Fehrenbach, T. R. *Lone Star*. New York: Macmillan Co., 1968.

Fowler, Mike. *Mini-Museum on the History of the Texas State Capitol*. Austin: Texas House of Representatives, 1981.

———. *Recommendations for Basic Improvements in the Public Halls of the Texas State Capitol Building, the Offices of the Texas House of Representatives, the Chamber of the House of Representatives, and Capitol Grounds*. Austin: Texas House of Representatives, 1984.

Friend, Llerena. *Sam Houston: The Great Designer*. Austin: University of Texas Press, 1964.

Hart, Katherine. *Austin and Travis County: A Pictorial History, 1839–1939*. Austin: Encino Press, 1975.

Holz, Robert K. et al. *Texas and Its History*. Austin and Dallas: Graphic Ideas, Inc., 1972.

Jones, Diane Susan. "The Preservation of the Texas Capitol." Master's thesis, University of Texas, 1980.

Kemp, L. W. "The Capitol (?) at Columbia." *Southwestern Historical Quarterly* 48, no. 1 (July 1944).

———. "A Capital Site." Washington-on-the-Brazos Star of the Republic Museum 6, no. 2 (Winter 1981).

Kingston, Michael T., ed. *Texas Almanac and State Industrial Guide, 1984–85*. Dallas: A. H. Belo Corp., 1983.

Maguire, Jack. *Texas: Amazing, but True*. Austin: Eakin Publications, Inc., 1984.

Moreland, Sinclair. *Governors' Messages: Coke to Ross, 1874–91*. Austin: Texas State Library, 1916.

Pool, William C. *Historical Atlas of Texas*. Austin: Encino Press, 1971.

Potts, Robert J., Jr. "Cloud Over the Capitol Grounds." *Texas Parade*, October 1963.

Rathjen, Frederick W. "The Texas Statehouse: A Study of the Building of the Texas Capitol Based on the Reports of the Capitol Building Commissioners." *Southwestern Historical Quarterly* 60, no. 4 (1957).

Richardson, Rupert N. *Texas: The Lone Star State*. Englewood Cliffs, N.J.: Prentice-Hall, Inc., 1981.

Roberts, O. M. "The Capitols of Texas." *Texas State Historical Association Quarterly* 2, no. 2 (October 1898).

Texas Centennial of Statehood Commission. *A Century of Texas Governors and Capitols*. Austin: June 14, 1943.

Texas Legislative Council. *The Texas Capitol: Symbol of Accomplishment*. Austin: Texas Department of Highways and Transportation, 1982.

Texas State Historical Association. *Texas History Illustrated*. Houston: *Houston Chronicle*, 1974.

Tolbert, Frank X. "Texas Capitols." (series) *Dallas Morning News*, July 1960.

Walsh, W. C. "Memories of a Land Commissioner." *Southwestern Historical Quarterly* 44, no. 4 (April 1941).

Webb, Walter P., and H. Bailey Carroll, eds. *The Handbook of Texas*. Austin: Texas State Historical Association, 1952.

Weddle, Robert S. "Granite Mountain: A Rock for a Horse." *Southwest Heritage*, December 1968.

Willoughby, Larry. *Austin: A Historical Portrait*. Norfolk, Va.: The Donning Co., 1981.

Winkler, Ernest William. "The Seat of Government in Texas." *Texas State Historical Association Quarterly* 10, no. 3, (January 1907).

Wortham, Louis J. *A History of Texas*. Fort Worth: Wortham-Molyneaux Co., 1924.

Newspapers:

Various issues of the *Austin American-Statesman, Austin Daily Tribune, Austin Democratic-Statesman, Texas Sentinel, Texas Siftings, Waco Day*, and others.

Magazines:

Southwest Airlines Magazine
Texas Highways
Texas Public Employee
Texas Architect
Texas Bar Journal

Index

Note: The abbreviation "cs" in index refers to color sections, listing page numbers in successive order.

The authors (standing left to right) Mike Fowler, Jack Maguire, Noel Grisham, and Marla Ragland Johnson (seated).

About the Authors

MIKE FOWLER

Mike Fowler worked for the Texas House of Representatives for fourteen years. After earning his bachelor of arts degree in government from The University of Texas at Austin in 1970, he started working in the House of Representatives, where he served as chief assistant sergeant-at-arms and property manager until he resigned in 1985. During his employment he was responsible for completing a mini-museum on the history of the Texas State Capitol, as well as numerous other exhibits. In 1986 Fowler was the Democratic candidate for state representative in Burnet and Williamson counties. He now serves as president of the Hutto Chamber of Commerce and is in his tenth year as a councilman for the City of Hutto.

JACK MAGUIRE

Jack Maguire makes his home in Fredericksburg after retiring as executive director of the Institute of Texan Cultures. He had formerly served as executive director of The University of Texas Ex-Students Association. He is author of six books on Texas, including his latest, *Texas, Amazing But True*.

NOEL GRISHAM

Noel Grisham, a former member of the Texas House of Representatives, was a public school superintendent for thirty-two years, the last twenty-two years in Round Rock Independent School District. He has been lieutenant governor of the Texas Oklahoma District of Kiwanis International and has served on several state committees. He is the author of numerous articles for state and national journals and has authored or co-authored seven books.

MARLA RAGLAND JOHNSON

Marla Ragland Johnson worked at the Capitol for three years after graduating with honors from Texas A&M University with a degree in journalism and health education. She is presently a full-time mother to her children, Wes and Krista, and a part-time student working toward certification as a certified public accountant. She and her husband, John, live in San Marcos, Texas.